**Branding Identity**
contemporary graphic design

First Published by Sendpoints Books
Copyright©2009

Published and distributed in Europe and Latin America by:

Index Book, SL
Consell de Cent, 160 local 3
08015 Barcelona, Spain
Phone: +34 93 454 5547
Fax: + 34 454 8438
ib@indexbook.com
www.indexbook.com

ISBN 978-84-96774-99-5

ACKNOWLEDGEMENTS

We would like to thank all the designers and companies
who made a significant contribution to the compilation of
this book. Without them, this project would not have been
possible.
We would also like to thank all the producers for their
invaluable assistance throughout. Its successful completion
also owes a great deal to many professionals in the
creative industry who have given us precious insights and
comments. We are also very grateful to many other people
whose names do not appear on the credits for making specific
input and continuous support the whole time.

**Branding Identity**
contemporary graphic design

# Branding Identity

What's in a brand name? Everything! Think of these brands: Coke, Barbie, Hershey, McDonalds, Madonna, Pepsi, Bono, Microsoft, Kleenex, Xerox, Steven Spielberg, Dell and GM. Did you notice that brands can be things, replicas of people and actual people? Brands are the public perception of a thing or person. Companies work very hard to establish their brand, sometimes failing when they attempt to tie a secondary product into the popular brand name. Does anyone even remember A1 chicken sauce?

The people and companies behind the above brand names are well known. They are established. They have earned the right to be positioned where they are in the public's eye. Are you or your products clearly associated with the solution you seek to provide? What about your products? What about your name? How are you positioned in the marketplace? As an entrepreneur, a small Businessperson, you have to be ever so keenly aware of every minute detail and opportunity to brand yourself. You need to be the expert. Your products must solve the problem, and the world needs to know about it. Branding therefore, may be the most important marketing challenge you face as your Business plan unfolds.

It's all about public perception. Is Coke the real thing? Does Hershey make the finest chocolate? Does McDonalds offer the best tasting, most nutritious hamburger? Does GM make the finest cars? We have been trained by skilled marketers to make the above associations. We have been conditioned over time to accept the advertising as real, whether we actually believe it or not. Very clever indeed, these makers have been. You cannot afford to be any less convincing in your efforts.

As CEO of your own organization, you will most likely not have the extensive resources that a major company or big name star has. You probably are the marketing department, the advertising department, the sales team, the accountant and so on. As such, you must remain acutely aware of your image, the perception of each and every customer, and to a great extent, the marketplace as a whole. Your position in the marketplace,

often dictated by the perceived quality of your products, your celebrity, your reputation for service, your leadership in your field and your consistency will certainly have a great deal to do with the effectiveness of your brand. You are the brand.

As the brand, you must take the position that you will always be under scrutiny, under the microscope. Assume leadership. You may not be the biggest guy in your field, but through leadership you can establish a market presence that will help you to become positioned along with the major players in your market. Take the lead on local issues or take a stand on a national issue that relates to your product, service and market. Through association, you will be perceived as a market leader, regardless of your size. Attempt to resolve a small problem and associate it with a greater one and you will achieve a level of notoriety, one that you can leverage to increase your brand awareness.

Your company must be credible. That is to say that your products and services must do what you say they will. You must also be credible personally. If you cannot be rightfully associated with your products or services offering, it will be difficult for the public to be receptive to such a contradiction. Honesty and integrity will be assets of great value to you as your marketplace gets to know you.

A logo design is composed of one or more elements of shape, type, and thematically chosen colors. In a glance, it conveys a substantial amount of information to the viewer, much in the form of short gut feelings that aren't vocalized -good, hesitant, authoritative, dignified, classy, upscale, expertise, cheap?the list is endless.

Your logo is a symbol that will stand on every piece of printed or electronic collateral for at least the next 10 years. Remember that thought. Changing your logo in a year because you don't like it breeds confusion and mistrust that spreads like weeds within your audience. Many people

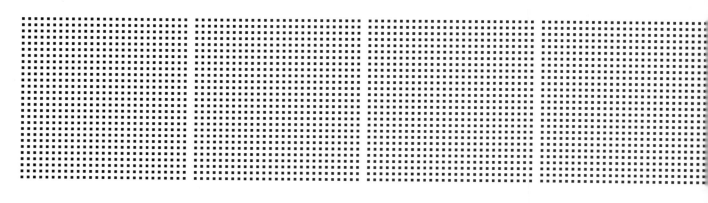

ver look that fact when they have a logo
esigned from the Internet for $25.

our identity is an extension of your
usiness that communicates visually,
hrough appearance, and emotionally,
hrough symbolism. Curtailing or ignoring
hought, revision, and growth in the design
rocess will hurt your finished product and
orporate image. A good graphic artist will
ead you through the design process. He or
he will help visualize your company as the
orld sees you.

I'm not creative," "I can't draw," "Make
t green cause green is my favorite color
nd I'm the boss and it's my logo!" If you
ind yourself thinking along these lines,
ou're pretty normal so don't worry! If
our passion and talent lie in matching the
erfect violin to a young blossoming talent
hat walks into your music store, you're
robably not going to do your own corporate
ax returns.

ou must be consistent. You must find your
iche, take your stance, establish some
osition and build from it. If you change
very week or every time a new wind blows,
eople will not take you seriously. They
ill begin to doubt your leadership and find
t difficult to perceive you as a credible
ource for your goods and services. You
ill lose whatever market position you have
ained and whatever leadership position that
ou have achieved by wobbling among various
irections. The public sees consistency as
trength and strength as character. When you
re a small company, struggling to grow, the
erception of you in the marketplace is a
ritical factor.

our marketing plan should certainly
nclude these concerns as well as the
ncredible importance of the awareness of
our market image. Since you are the brand,
ew components within your Business plan
hould receive more of your attention than
he development of the public's perception
f you, your evolving position in the
arketplace and the development of your
rand image.

### Strategy and Tips for a Successful Logo Design

Visual processing is the most important way for gathering information for all human beings. A good design or graphics work is remembered for ages and that is what drives the multinational companies to spend millions of dollars on developing their logo and other branding material. They would go to any extent to create a solid visual impact and leave a permanent impression on their customer's mind.

While designing your logo and providing the necessary details to your designer you need to always keep in mind what you want your customers to feel about your company when the see your logo. A logo design can actually be a compressed story for your business and tell your customers about the nature and attitude of your Business.

### "Logo Design" Begins at Home

Yes, your home is the place where you take the first step of your logo design process. Look at the different bottles and pouches you are using everyday in the kitchen, look at the logos they have, look at the logos on your electronic equipments, check the logo on the bag that you got from the shopping mall yesterday. Everyday we come across thousands of logos but we remember just a few, if we look around, we can find different types of logos around us. Also, visit the local supermarket to check the logos on the array of products they have. It is always better to check out the logos of your competitors who are in the same industry. While doing this, you are sure to find some logos that stand out from the others and this is going to help you conceptualize your logo design.

Once you have made up your mind on how you want your logo to be, its time you write them down clearly demarcated into small objective points which can work as instructions for your logo designer.

One thing you should be careful, while going through different logos of other companies you must not be so influenced by any of them so that your logo becomes a replica or modified version of another logo that you saw. A good design often affects our sub conscious mind and we unknowingly duplicate

certain parts of it. It is extremely important that your logo design is unique. A unique logo design increases the likelihood for getting a trademark protection. It is advisable that you take the assistance of a trademark lawyer for your trademark search and to ensure that you do not run into the risk of infringing some other companies trademark symbol or logo.

### Using Clip Art

If you are a small local Business or a mom-n-pop shop you might not be that keen in investing towards a logo and establishing your brand (though I sincerely believe that's very wrong). In such situation, you can try using some high quality royalty free clip art combining it with a suitable typeface to put your company name. You can also use more than one clip arts to create the total graphics for your logo.

However, you should keep in mind that clip arts would never give you the effect of a custom logo and they can be easily duplicated or stolen. Even if you are modifying a clip art, it is almost impossible to get a trademark on that. In future, once your Business grows to the level when you need to have trademarked logo you will have to get a total new logo (may be something closer to the one you have) an start with your branding efforts once again to establish that new logo.

To avoid all this problems it is advisable that you get a unique custom logo and it is not always that you need to spend a lot on your logos. There are companies on the web that offers custom logo design at reasonabl price.

### Some More Logo Design Tips

1) **Keep it simple:** Remember, simplicity is the key. Most of the great logos are absolutely simple and it is always easier for us to remember and recognize a simple design than to identify a complicated artwork. If you want to have some complex illustration for your logo, try to minimize the number of lines and make it as simple as possible keeping in mind that the viewer should be able to understand what has been drawn.

"Re-branding is an
incredibly
difficult and at times
frustrating
process to get through,
especially if you are doing
it for
the first time..."

**Typography:** You should be careful while
deciding on the typeface that you intend
to use for your logo. Choosing the correct
typeface can make a lot of difference.
For example, a finance company depicting
strength and stability would like to use
some bold, thick font. Also, the letters can
be twisted to create simple yet nice logos.
Some ideal examples of logo that contains
only letters are "SONY" and Dell - remember
the twisted "e"?

**Always Use Vector Graphics:** Always ask
your designer to provide you the logo as
vector graphics. The advantage is, vector
graphics can be resized without any loss of
details and image quality. You can resize it
as per your requirement. In addition, vector
graphics take lesser memory capacity in your
computer.

**Choice of Color:** You should be careful
while deciding on your logo colors. It is
advisable to restrict yourself to RGB or
CMYK colors so that your logo looks equally
good in print as it looks on web. Also,
ensure that your logo looks good in black
and white as well, mind it, you will also
have to use your logo on while faxing any
of your marketing material or corporate
documents.

Finally, it is always better if you are
employing any specialized logo design firm
to create your logo design than doing it
yourself. It is their profession so they
would know it much better than you do and
neither is logo design always very costly.
Definitely, there are companies that charge
you $500 for a logo, however there are
also companies that offers equally good
services with very much affordable pricing
(Corporate Logo Design). It is just a matter
of locating that designer and you can be on
your way to having a wonderful custom logo
design.

# WORKS

# Kalendar

Graphic designer Sander Tielen used the versatility of the digital numeral "8," creating different colored cards that slide in behind a black front to display the date with an appealingly clean retro '80s look. The number on the lower right hand corner in white indicates the month while the bright shading colors mark the day. Easy to use and read, all other calendars start to pale in comparison.

T: Tielen perpetual
   calendar
L: Drukkerij Tielen
F: Sander Tielen
D: Sander Tielen
E: Sander Tielen
M: photographer
O: Netherlands

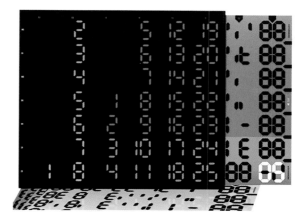

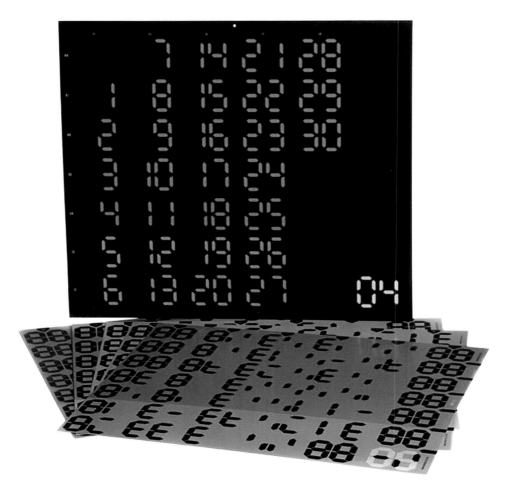

# Climate

Ökostrom what does that mean?
Under green electricity is electricity from renewables and won us unlimited and climate available. Green electricity from wind energy, solar energy, hydropower, geothermal and biomass. In addition stream of highly efficient cogeneration plants.

Local organisations responsible for protecting the climate commitment, there are many. Here in Munich, for example, there are zero degrees plus "an initiative by Green City Association, which set itself the goal has to act now and work together to stop the Erderwärmung.

---

TI: Environmental use
    in your region
CO: Germany

Stoppen wir die Erderwärmung.

# Identity

While crafting the visual identity for Emblem, we tried to offer an inside perspective of the brand. Being the best of both worlds, the brand is offering fashion design accompanied by graphic design and art direction. It's not a combination encountered too often in clothing lines. For the visuals we used a pigeons and leafs motif, that would suggest nature, paradise, positive thinking, beautiful, two in one. The pigeons shapes form a heart that is symbolizing love and passion, with different sense of color and even fabric present in the ID.

Emblem is a fashion brand for the high end market; a clothing line for DJs, different artists, people that go to expensive clubs, or people conscious about trends. It is made for people that are willing to spend more than average on their look-and-feel. We associated the brand with a certain lifestyle: the message is that Emblem gives you more personality, makes you look better, gives you style, makes you look smarter, and lets others know details are important to you. Emblem helps people help themselves by providing the means to express their personality.

TI: Launch Campaign
CL: Emblem Fashion Company
DF: Okapi Studio
CD: Gabi Lungu

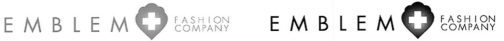

*Prepare to be seen differently*

*Prepare to be seen differently*

# Music

To design the cover for Grasu XXL's upcoming album, we had to bring together both the artist's image as well as his songs feelings into perfect graphic communication that would make the disc recognizable on the vendors' stands alongside other musical records. Being an upcoming artist, we realized people need to associate a face with the sounds they hear when they play it. We focused on his look and appeal, using photos and light graphic details to create the atmosphere. This is a project where graphics need to give a visual shape to the audio content. We took the project from scratch after a short briefing and project planning, starting with an in-house photo session. That was followed by the graphical process, and you can see the result bellow. We are looking forward to future similar projects because music is a big part of our lives.

TI: "Curaj" Cover
DF: Okapi Studio
CD: Gabi Lungu

# Advertise

DJ Swamp and Grasu XXL put their skills together a month ago and delivered a fine mixtape encompassing talents from various artists. The mashup contains new singles, remixes of old songs and cool collabs. We were commissioned for the graphical concept of this project, and we worked from scratch providing the direction, photo shootings, graphic edits, for their covers, landing page and advertising.

TI: Evident Mixtape - Grasu XXL & DJ Swamp
DF: Okapi Studio
CD: Gabi Lungu

Dana Nicolescu / 0722 225502 / its@sunnyday.ro

# Card

Okapi built from
scratch the Sunnyday
brand by associating
the nice t-shirts with
the sunny days when
people are wearing
them. The audience is
18 to 40 years old. In
a saturated market with
many good players, by
using a simple strategy
and playful visuals,
we created the perfect
start for this small
business. We all wish
you a Sunnyday!

CL: Sunnyday Clothing
    Company
DF: Okapi Studio
CD: Gabi Lungu

# Estate

After being on the market for 2 years, Terracan realized their communication was not reflecting the current reality of the company. We had to give shape to their brand identity. The minimalistic approach of the cube styled shape we used for the logo was meant to showcase the idea of space, as well as the innovative and fresh business approach of this real estate agency. Terracan deals with the luxury market real estate, mostly characterized by affordable large spaces. Before we met their campaigns were solely focused on direct selling with ads showcasing houses and pricing information. Our task was to promote more the company and the brand than the current available buildings offer. The "bigger houses" campaign proved to be effective in communicating their services.

---

CL: Terracan Real Estate
DF: Okapi Studio
CD: Gabi Lungu

bigger houses

bigger houses

FLORIN COLCERU
LOGISTICS DIRECTOR
tel: 021.326.55.60, fax: 021.323.73.51, mobil: 0723.361.821,
e-mail: florin.colceru@terracan.ro

Bd. Corneliu Coposu 5, bl. 103, sc. 2, ap.28
Sector 3, Bucuresti

www.terracan.ro

# Books

In general the banks are associated with a cold, serious image, we tried to differentiate this HVB project by designing a friendly looking approach and at the same time keeping their corporate aspect. You wouldn`t want your clients, partners or employees to shove down your documents in the deepest corner of their cabinet and forget them there. You want your documents to to be pleasant and good looking when they are presented, and to stand up when they are on a table together with other ones.

---

TI: Friendly folders
CL: HVB Group
DF: Okapi Studio
CD: Gabi Lungu

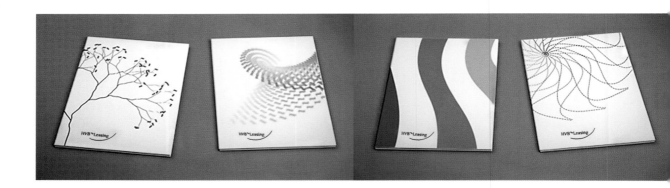

# Award

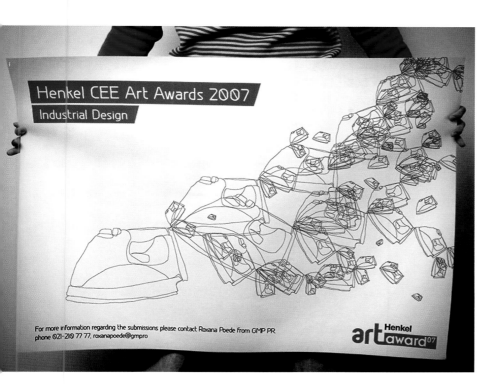

Henkel is a leader with brands and technologies that make people's lives easier, better and more beautiful. They are holding an industrial design contest in 2007 in Vienna, Austria gathering talents and ideas from all over Eastern Europe. We made the print communication for the event, clearly expressing the industrial theme, offering simplicity and the feeling that ideas can spread fast.

CL: Henkel CEE Art
    Awards
DF: Okapi Studio
CD: Gabi Lungu
YP: 2007

# Posters

We made this two prints for the PostIndustrial competition organized by HyperWerk FHBB Department of the Swiss University of Applied Sciences. The theme was called "What should post industrial design do?". Both prints are finalists in the contest.

TI: HyperWerk FHBB
DF: Okapi Studio
CD: Gabi Lungu

# Posters

Crize is a young fresh rock band. Their true fans are the young kind that you see running around on skates and bikes all summer long. The chosen visual style is the thing that catches their attention making the curious. It stands up when it is placed on walls full of posters and graffiti because of its colorful and high toned nature.

C: Crize Band
F: Okapi Studio
D: Gabi Lungu

# Magazine

Floe magazine is gathering 130 pages of fashion, architecture, interior design, music, movies, and photo essays, by promoting an intelligent lifestyle concept. With this concept, it positions itself in the Canadian market without having any direct competition. Our target audience for this project is 60% women and 40% men, who are intelligent, sophisticated, and enjoy the finer things in life. They know the difference between quality and cheap stuff; they want a magazine to read for pleasure and not for financial or politic information. The producers made sure that the editors would be Canadian stars, and that the paper and printing process would have the best quality. Before designing Flow magazine, we started with the branding process. The solution offered is based on custom made typography. The cursive font with curved shapes, influenced by modern design, is easy to read, and being the fact that Floe is a young upcoming magazine, we choused to position the logotype on the header, large with white background, so people can notice it fast at the news stand.

CL: Floe Magazine
DF: Okapi Studio
CD: Gabi Lungu

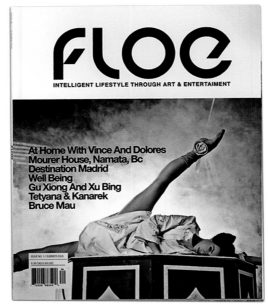

# Concept

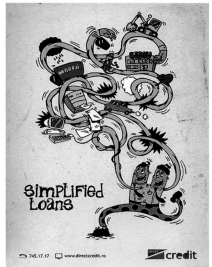

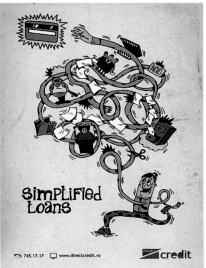

Direct Credit, a credit brokerage and consulting company, approached Okapi in order to solve a communication problem that they were facing. This is a unique business, offering custom built packages for each one's needs, by first studying the market and the available offers and then serving directions to the ones looking for credit. While they are offering a large pool of services, there was a need to differentiate clearly each type of credit package, with it's features and benefits. We got the customer involved in the picture, making up little relevant stories about the good and the bad parts of searching for the perfect credit.

TI: Things Can Be
    Easier
CL: Direct Credit
DF: Okapi Studio
CD: Gabi Lungu

# Identity

Claystone Farms is a new horseback riding and horse boarding facility in the Grand Rapids, MI area. Claystone's owners wanted a very graphic appearance and chose a deep purple combined with metallic copper inks. The customer wanted to use a horse head in their new logo design. I presented four concepts and the one depicted here was chosen. U.S. Postal approval was aquired in order to fulfill the customer's request of printing their logo over the window of their envelope.

---

TI: Two-color Corporate
    Identity package
CL: Claystone Fams
CO: USA

# Clothing

C: Shelli Jin
F: DesignDo brand
   design consulting
   organization
D: Long Gang
   Li Jiong
D: Long Gang
   Li Jiong
E: Long Gang
   Li Jiong
D: China

# Visual

CL: BELAND
DF: DesignDo brand
    design consulting
    organization
CD: Long Gang
    Li Jiong
AD: Long Gang
    Li Jiong
DE: Long Gang
    Li Jiong
CO: China

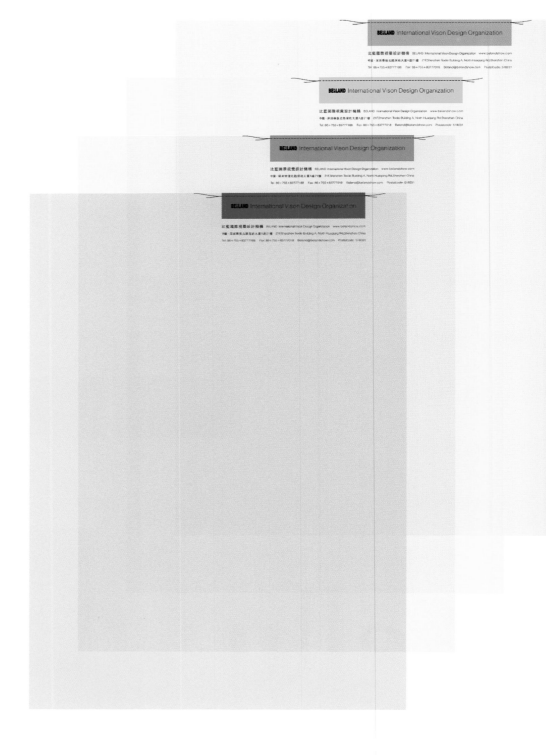

**BE:LAND** International Vison Design Organization

比藍國際視覺設計機構 BELAND International Vison Design Organization www.belandshow.com
中國 · 深圳車強北路深紡大廈A座21樓 21F.Shenzhen Textile Building A, North Huaqiang Rd,Shenzhen China
Tel: 86+755+83777188 Fax: 86+755+83777018 Beland@belandshow.com Postalcode: 518031

**BE:LAND** International Vison Design Organization

比藍國際視覺設計機構 BELAND International Vison Design Organization www.belandshow.com
中國 · 深圳車強北路深紡大廈A座21樓 21F.Shenzhen Textile Building A, North Huaqiang Rd,Shenzhen China
Tel: 86+755+83777188 Fax: 86+755+83777018 Beland@belandshow.com Postalcode: 518031

**BE:LAND** International Vison Design Organization

比藍國際視覺設計機構 BELAND International Vison Design Organization www.belandshow.com
中國 · 深圳車強北路深紡大廈A座21樓 21F.Shenzhen Textile Building A, North Huaqiang Rd,Shenzhen China
Tel: 86+755+83777188 Fax: 86+755+83777018 Beland@belandshow.com Postalcode: 518031

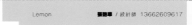

**BE:LAND** International Vison Design Organization

比藍國際視覺設計機構 BELAND International Vison Design Organization www.belandshow.com
中國 · 深圳車強北路深紡大廈A座21樓 21F.Shenzhen Textile Building A, North Huaqiang Rd,Shenzhen China
Tel: 86+755+83777188 Fax: 86+755+83777018 Beland@belandshow.com Postalcode: 518031

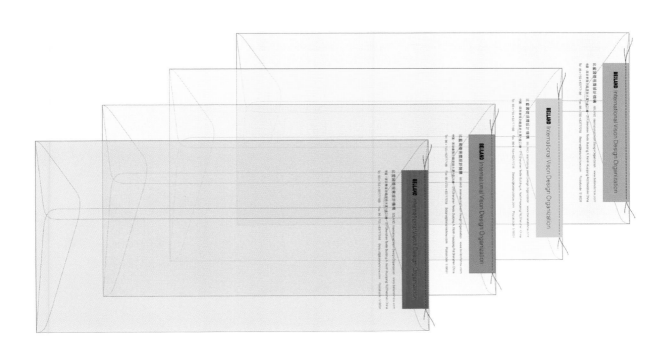

# Company

CL: DesignDo brand
    design consulting
    organization
DF: DesignDo brand
    design consulting
    organization
CD: Long Gang
    Li Jiong
AD: Long Gang
    Li Jiong
DE: Long Gang
    Li Jiong
CO: China

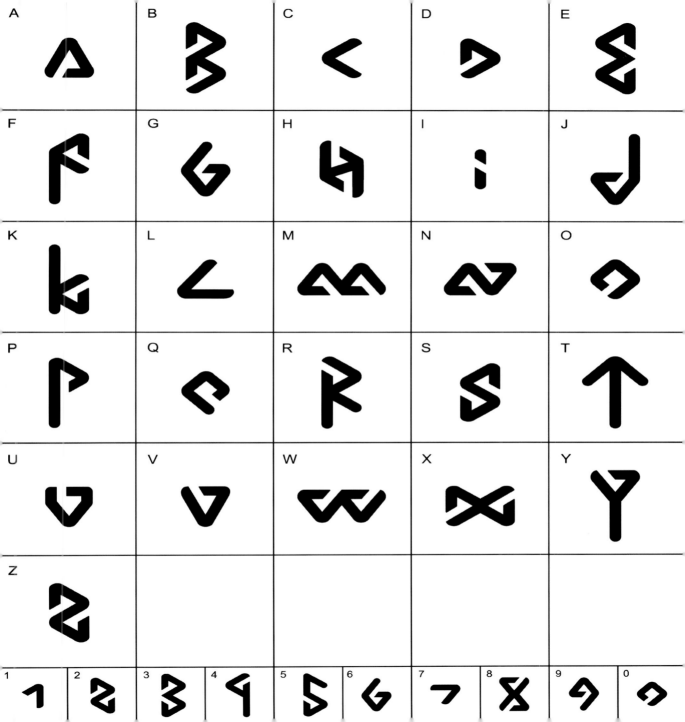

# OwnBrand

TI: Tangram
DF: DesignDo brand
    design consulting
    organization
CD: Long Gang
    Li Jiong
AD: Long Gang
    Li Jiong
DE: Long Gang
    Li Jiong
CO: China

taurant

KI Hotel
signDo brand
sign consulting
ganization
ng Gang
  Jiong
ng Gang
  Jiong
ng Gang
  Jiong
ina

*Everywhere is*
# KIKI™

*Everywhere is*
**KIKI**™

*Everywhere is*
**KIKI**™

*Everywhere is*
**KIKI**™

*Everywhere is*
**KIKI**™

*Everywhere is*
**KIKI**™

*Everywhere is*
**KIKI**™

*Everywhere is*
**KIKI**™

*Everywhere is*
**KIKI**™

*Everywhere is*
**KIKI**™

*Everywhere is*
**KIKI**™

*Everywhere is*
**KIKI**™

*Everywhere is*
**KIKI**™

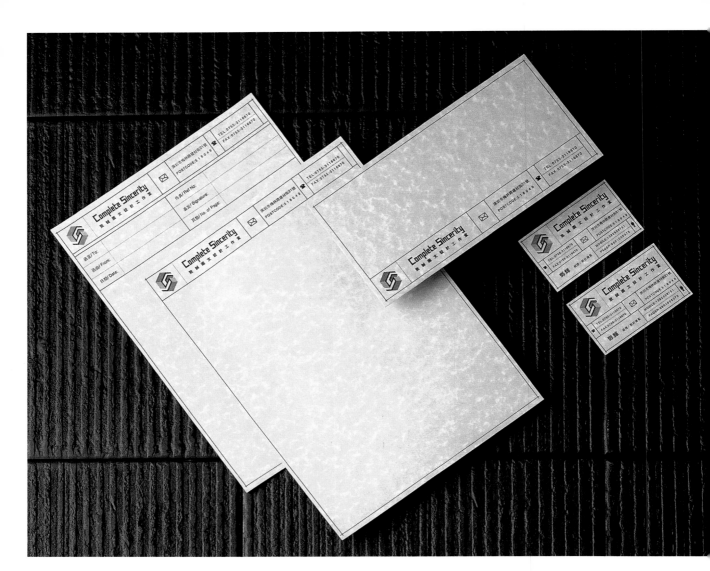

# Studio

CL: Complete Sincerity
DF: DesignDo brand
    design consulting
    organization
CD: Long Gang
    Li Jiong
AD: Long Gang
    Li Jiong
DE: Long Gang
    Li Jiong
CO: China

Bar

L: Face Bar
F: DesignDo brand
   design consulting
   organization
D: Long Gang
   Li Jiong
D: Long Gang
   Li Jiong
E: Long Gang
   Li Jiong
O: China

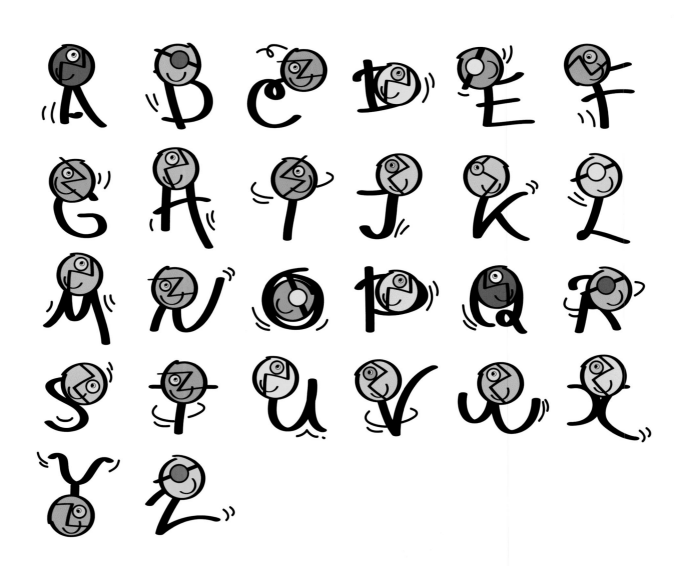

当夜幕悄然而至的时候,千里光FACE BAR便渐渐活跃,激昂跳跃的DJ音乐带来了无限的热情和活力、千里光FACE BAR········面对面　地址:　重庆万州区白岩路440号华顺购物广场二楼　电话: 86 023 58290000

# OwnBrand

TI: Cars appear to
DF: DesignDo brand
    design consulting
    organization
CD: Long Gang
    Li Jiong
AD: Long Gang
    Li Jiong
DE: Long Gang
    Li Jiong
CO: China

# Imprint

TI: I'M XXX my card
DF: DesignDo brand
    design consulting
    organization
CD: Long Gang
    Li Jiong
AD: Long Gang
    Li Jiong
DE: Long Gang
    Li Jiong
CO: China

# i'm xxx

i'mxxx i'mooo i'mzzz i'm◇◇◇ i'mooo
i'm⊐⊐⊐ i'm∗∗∗ i'm※※※ i'm∧∧∧ i'm◁◁◁
i'mccc i'm### i'm✿✿✿ i'm<<< i'm÷÷÷
i'm△△△ i'm+++ i'm$$$ i'm\\\ i'm□□□
i'm▽▽▽ i'm___ i'mvvv i'm□□□ i'm///
i'm▷▷▷ i'm=== i'm✕✕✕ i'm>>> i'm???

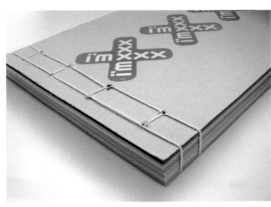

# Exhibition

TI: I'M XXX my card
DF: DesignDo brand
    design consulting
    organization
CD: Long Gang
    Li Jiong
AD: Long Gang
    Li Jiong
DE: Long Gang
    Li Jiong
CO: China

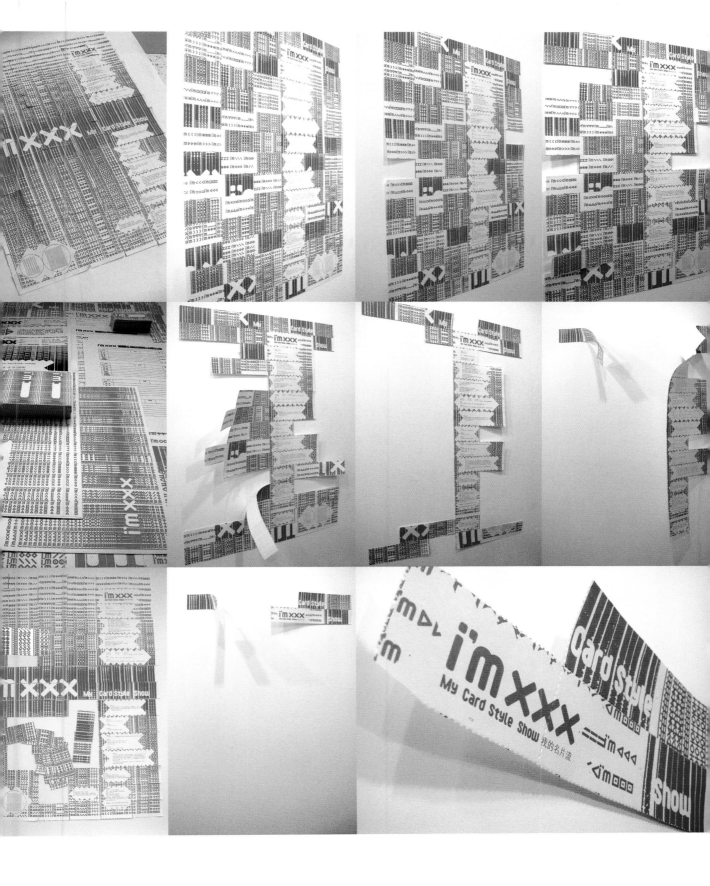

# Rock

TI: VIVA Rock
DF: DesignDo brand
    design consulting
    organization
CD: Long Gang
    Li Jiong
AD: Long Gang
    Li Jiong
DE: Long Gang
    Li Jiong
CO: China

# XiaoLong

CL: XiaoLong Music
    Studio
DF: DesignDo brand
    design consulting
    organization
CD: Long Gang
    Li Jiong
AD: Long Gang
    Li Jiong
DE: Long Gang
    Li Jiong
CO: China

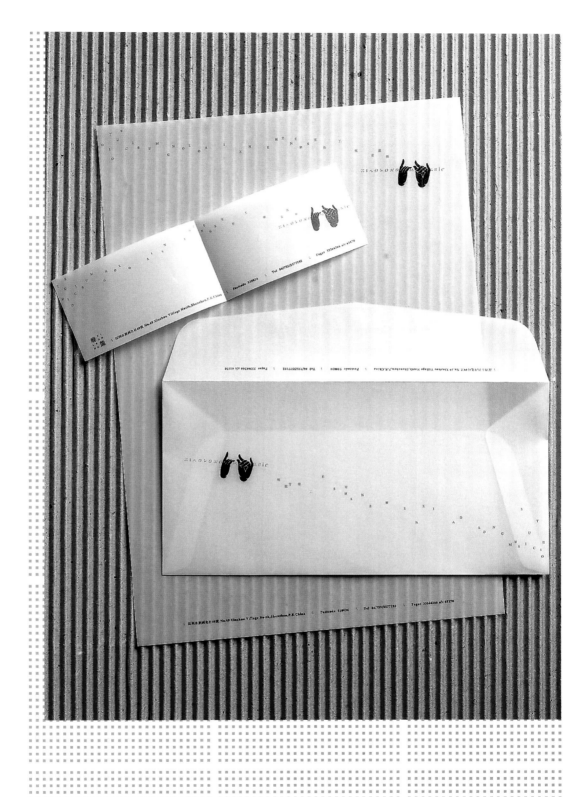

# Utility

Core is one of the UK's leading utility suppliers. Gas, electricity, telecoms and water delivered in one package. Their existing identity was old, tired and fragmented, failing to reflect their multiple offering and the energy and commitment of a new management team. We created a new mark that pulled the company together under one banner, whilst offering the flexibility for each division to differentiate itself if necessary.

---

CL: Core

**AT CORE WE VALUE
YOUR OPINION
AS MUCH AS
YOUR BUSINESS**

**WITH A DEDICATED
PROJECT MANAGER FOR
EVERY DEVELOPMENT,
THE BUCK STOPS HERE.**

**ONE TEAM, MULTI UTILITIES.
SOMETIMES THE SIMPLEST
IDEAS ARE THE BEST.**

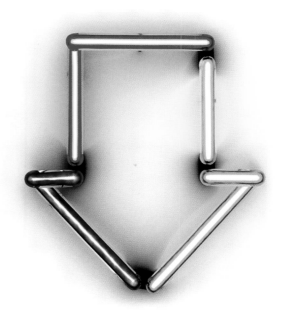

# Buses

Utilising Arriva's existing guidelines and with a limited budget, we created a new name and individual style, using colour, language and iconography to attract attention, inform and drive footfall on the new service. Posters, banners, leaflets, tickets, uniforms and ultimately the design of the new buses have all fallen under our remit. Not only that, our thorough approach has led us to look at a totally new 'West of Scotland' look and feel for all deliverables across all services. We've never seen as many buses as we do now!

Arriva is Europe's biggest public transport provider so it was good news when they approached us to brand their new express service between Glasgow Airport and the city centre.

CL: Arriva

Friendly advice from someone I can trust

mutual**benefit**

skipton.co.uk
0845 60 40 400*

mutual**matters** SKIPTON BUILDING SOCIETY

to re-brand, but were understandably nervous about the whole process. We worked closely with an incumbent agency who they trusted implicitly and the results speak for themselves. Skipton already had a brand, it was in their people and their branches, personal and honest advice, all we needed to do was to bring this alive in their communications.

CL: Skipton

**mortgages**
We've found our dream home, now we need the perfect mortgage

**home insurance**
We want taking out cover to be simple

skipton.co.uk

mutual**matters** SKIPTON

NORWICH UNION    mutual**matters** SKIPTON

**Branch Access Account**

**4.85**% gross p.a.
**4.60**% AER

including a 0.5% bonus for the first six months

• Easy penalty free access
• Friendly in branch service

Open a Branch Access Account
**face-to-face** today

**mortgages**
We think they should be explained in plain English

skipton.co.uk    mutual**matters** SKIPTON

JCDecaux

Someone knowing my face matters

mutual**understanding**

0845 60 40 400*

matters SKIPTON

# Cheeses

Previous packs offered no differentiation from supermarket own label, and didn't reflect the artisan nature of the creameries that actually made the cheese. Hidden away in isolated sites on the west coast of Scotland, the smallest of the creameries has only six staff. We immediately created a company name and a new mark to encompass the collection, with Scotland playing a key role in the markings on our cow. From the materials for the new packs to the typography and new illustrations by Iain Macintosh, everything was created to reflect the hand finished quality of the products.

CL: The Scottish
    Highlands & Islands
    Cheese Company

Black Bottle needed a campaign to raise awareness of the brand. Our research led us to the conclusion that we needed to be bold to stand out form the humdrum of samey whisky promotions. Black Bottle is unique in that it is the only blend of the seven Islay malts. Strangely it actually comes in a green bottle and amongst the plethora of blends its award winning taste is unmistakable. All in all pretty unconventional. This allowed us to have some fun, stand out from the crowd and grab some serious attention.

CL: Black Bottle

# Utility

We really try to avoid free pitching when we can, but once in a while something comes along that you can't ignore. Bacardi Global Brands' William Lawson's Scotch Whisky repackaging project was one such pitch. A big export brand, shifting well over 1M cases in mainland Europe annually, it was a big challenge and one we were well up for. The eureka moment came when we realised we could reduce everything the brand stood for down to a single platform from which all other brand elements could be rebuilt and refreshed – from typography to iconography. It worked. Everyone who saw it got it and although this platform has since been refined and developed, it was certainly this holistic approach that won us the pitch. Since then, we've had the opportunity to take it further than just the pack: currently in publication is a whole new below the line look and feel for the brand in Europe. The end product 18 months later is a new look evolution of the old pack: bolder, sleeker and more elegant but still unmistakably William Lawson's.

CL: William Lawson's

# Product

Equal Exchange is a workers co-operative who bring the world's finest organic and fairtrade products to the UK. With limited budget and no above the line support the packs have a huge job to do. Our response was to use tongue in cheek copy to talk frankly to the consumer about the three main benefits of buying Equal Exchange products. With over 67 sku's, it was a copywriters nightmare to ensure every pack was not only different, but reflected each individual product.

CL: Equal Exchange

# Cashmere

Pure Collection is the
UK's leading online
cashmere retailer.
The owners of the
business are immensely
passionate about every
detail and we took the
same care and approach
to their brand. At the
heart of it all, we
combined the two halves
of the company. English
heritage and reserve,
from their home in
Harrogate, combined
with the colour and
passion of Mongolia,
where they gather and
manufacture the finest
of cashmere. A line from
the brief, 'Elegance
With A Twist', gave
us our vision for the
brand and we created
a series of Mongolian
influenced ribbons to
complement the dark
browns and greens of a
quintessential England,
to form the backbone of
the brand and all its
deliverables.

CL: Pure Collection

One Hundred Pounds Gift Voucher

Everyone loves to receive cashmere as a gift and we hope that you will e...
spending the enclosed voucher. The best thing about receiving Pure Coll...
Gift Vouchers is that they always come in the right style, colour and size. You can
use part of the value of this voucher and bank the rest, or throw caution to the
wind and add to the value to get the garments you want. To redeem your voucher
just call our customer service team on the relevant number on the reverse, and
we will do the rest. Please have your voucher number to hand when placing your order.

To Helen Forbes
From Nick Falkingham

DATE ISSUED 17/01/07     VOUCHER NUMBER 782466

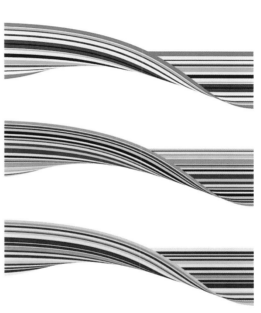

# Cashmere

Hungrys specialises in quality food for parties and corporate events. While meeting to discuss new photography for their website we uncovered the name of their holding company, The Really Delicious Food Company. We really felt this was the way forward for Hungrys and invested in some pro-active work to show the management team our vision. Luckily for us they loved the concepts and found some budget to make it a reality.

---

CL: Hungrys

I'M REALLY HANDY

THE REALLY DELICIOUS FOOD COMPANY
REALLY-DELICIOUS.COM

WE REALLY HOPE YOU ENJOY THIS

ORDER NUMBER

2968

CUSTOMER NAME

Jenny Aclap

Keep refrigerated or eat within 90 minutes of delivery. Please note food items may contain nuts or traces of nuts.

REALLY-DELICIOUS.CO

FOR A REALLY FRIENDLY CHAT WITH
MURRAY MCNICOL
07717 835 490
MURRAY.MCNICOL@REALLY-DELICIOUS.COM
REALLY-DELICIOUS.COM
32 WEST STREET · GLASGOW · G5 8RR
THE REALLY DELICIOUS FOOD CO. LTD T:0141 418 0202

THE REALLY DELICIOUS FOOD COMPANY

THE REALLY DELICIOUS FOOD COMPANY

REALLY EASY TO ORDER · REALLY FILLING · REALLY GOOD VALUE
FINGER, FORK AND FORMAL FOOD
FOR MEETINGS, PARTIES & SO MUCH MORE
DELIVERED TO YOUR OFFICE OR HOME & ALWAYS
TO YOUR DOOR
VISIT REALLY-DELICIOUS.COM

# Tomorrow

TI: GOLDEN HOME
CL: Vanke
DF: BOB Advertising
CD: Xia TianJian
AD: Su Yi
DE: Liu Ying
CO: China

Fashion Flare
Urban Chic
À la mode
Fashion Senses
Simply Style
Très Chic
Fashion Direction
Prêt a Porter
Glamour
Beauté

For Tomorrow

For Tomorrow

# Grid

TI: MEILONGZHEN
DF: BOB Advertising
CD: Liang Feng
    Wang Hong
AD: Liang Feng
    Wang Hong
DE: WU WeiXi
CO: China

金地梅陇镇™

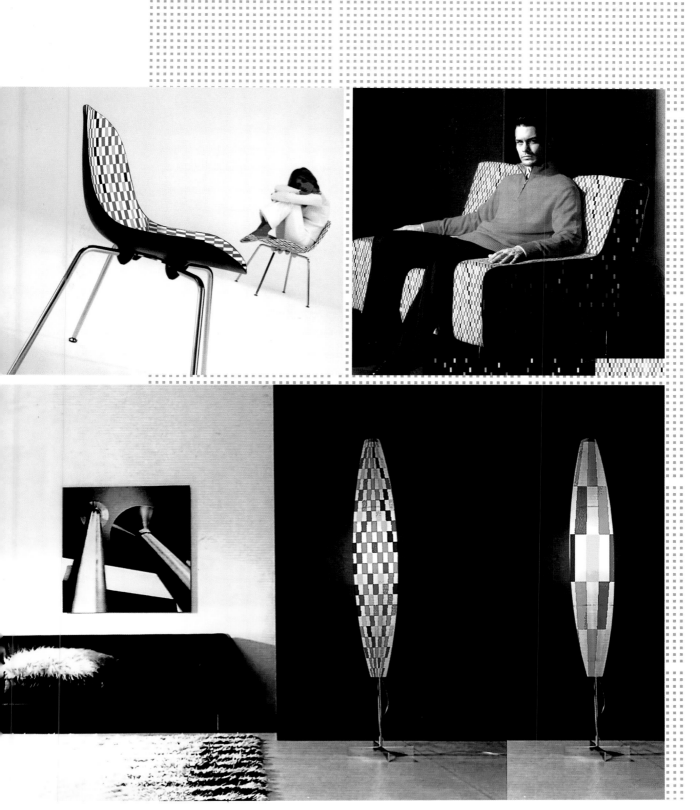

# Valley

TI: MONT Orchid Riverlet
DF: BOB Advertising
CD: Xia TianJian
AD: Su Yi
DE: Liu Ying
CO: China

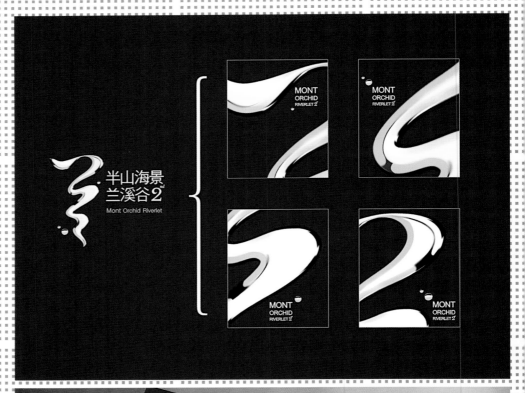

# Tape

Laboratorium is an outstanding design studio from Zagreb, Croatia.
Last year they created this simple calendar that can be put together by joining two adhesive tapes. As long as you put the right day on the first of each month, then you're safe. It's simple, smart and echo-friendly.

---

TI: Everlasting adhesive
    calendar
CL: Laboratorium
DF: Laboratorium
CD: Ivana Vucic,
    Orsat Frankovic
AD: Ivana Vucic
    Orsat Frankovic
DE: Ivana Vucic
    Orsat Frankovic
CO: Croatia
YP: 2007

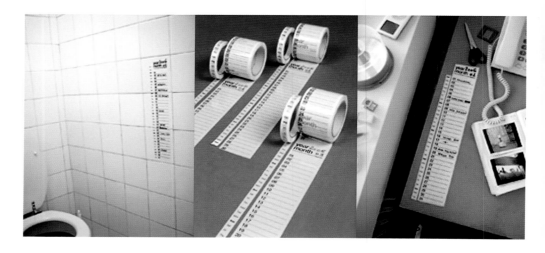

# Poster

I suppose that all those who have given you a paseillo through the centre of Madrid, habréis he noticed the existence of a series of posters published by the National Drama Center, a style quite appealing. We are fortunate to be able to observe on the website of that institution, but is missing some button to download it in a size a little more generous, for what we can track more closely, Hot Topic is not what anyone has swallowed me consists.
The work is the complete development of the theater programming of the National Theater during the season the 2007. Work has been selected by the Visual magazine.

TI: Centro Dramático
    Nacional
CL: CDN
DF: Isidro Ferrer
    asociados
CD: Isidro Ferrer
    Nicolás Sánchez
AD: Isidro Ferrer
    Nicolás Sánchez
DE: Isidro Ferrer
    Nicolás Sánchez
CO: Spain
YP: 2007

**CENTRO DRAMÁTICO NACIONAL**

DIRECCIÓN
**GERARDO VERA**

# ANTE LA JUBILACIÓN

DE **THOMAS BERNHARD**

TRADUCCIÓN
**MIGUEL SÁENZ**
DIRECCIÓN
**CARME PORTACELI**

**DEL 21 DE FEBRERO
AL 6 DE ABRIL
DE 2008**

REPARTO
POR ORDEN ALFABÉTICO
**TERESA LOZANO
GLORIA MUÑOZ
WALTER VIDARTE**

MOVIMIENTO
**MARTA CARRASCO**
ESPACIO ESCÉNICO E ILUMINACIÓN
**PACO AZORÍN**
VESTUARIO
**ANTONIO BELART**
BANDA SONORA
**JOSÉ ANTONIO GUTIÉRREZ "GUTI"**

GOBIERNO
DE ESPAÑA

MINISTERIO
DE CULTURA

INSTITUTO NACIONAL
DE LAS ARTES
ESCÉNICAS
Y DE LA MÚSICA

http://cdn.mcu.es
**VENTA TELEFÓNICA SERVICAIXA 902.33.22.11**

# Remember

Graphic design, which evokes emotions and for the benefit of customers still long in the mind of the beholder. The main basis for this are unconventional ideas and the courage to irritation. This is done mainly in the areas of corporate design, editorial design and graphic design. In addition to the daily business is a lot of time and heart blood in free, experimental projects invested.

---

TI: Tape to remember us
CL: Merkwürdig GmbH
DF: Merkwürdig GmbH
DE: Nadine Häfner
    Jennifer Staudacher
    Kai Staudacher
CO: Germany
YP: 2007

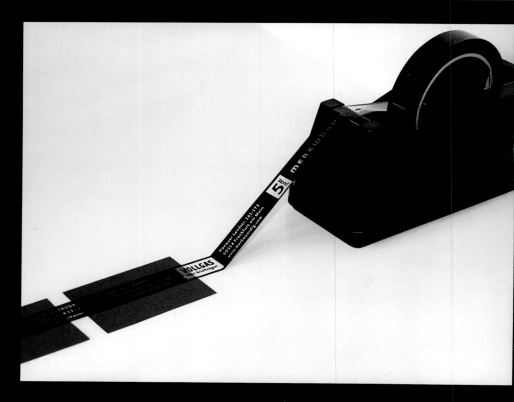

# Casarotto Ramsay &Associates

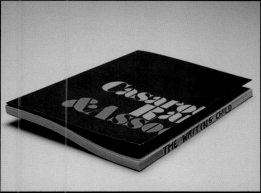

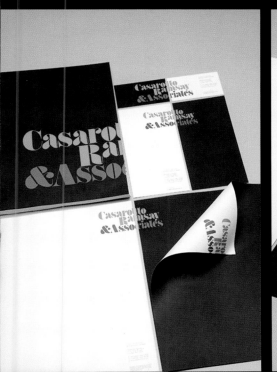

Jenne and Giorgio Casarotto founded the Casarotto Company in 1989 and in 1992 they joined forces with Tom Erhardt, former colleague of the late Peggy Ramsay, to create a bigger agency with an enviable client list. Because the company's identity was stuck in the past and Odd were commissioned to bring it into the 21st century - to convey the aspirational value and contemporary status expected of such a high-profile player within the sector. With a history spanning several significant creative and cultural era's, we thought the 1970's provided the broadest emotional connection to Casarotto's client base. We developed a primary typeface based on an original from the same era - reborn in 2006, with a modern twist and able to stand the test of time. So well known is Casarotto, we also decided to slice the logo between the front and back of the stationary - the first few letters enough to recognize the name and the cut a confident and bold statement to the competition.

CL: Casarotto Ramsay &
    Associates
DF: Odd
CD: Simon Glover
    Nick Stickland
AD: Stuart Bailey
    Richard Stevens
DE: Stuart Bailey
    Richard Stevens
CO: UK
YP: 2007

# Experiential

The box was sent to 50 of London's key celebrities, each one containing several pieces of inspirational communication. Firstly an iPod Nano, each containing a personalised video message from 'Q', the store concierge with an introduction to the iD, the store and its services and instructions as to how to book a free consultation. Then, an invitation to the launch party. Finally a set of 3 aluminium 'cube keys', each one crash numbered with 1 of 1000 unique codes. ODD also designed and produced 3 large-scale street cubes that were placed in high-traffic locations around London over a 2-week period. They replaced traditional media and advertising and featured short films and animations of real customers and the shoes that they made. In addition the cube contained 12,000 further unique codes that were distributed in a Bluetooth lottery that took place every 5mins throughout the day and night, giving winners from the public a chance to book in for an appointment with a consultant at the Nike iD Studio.

CL: Nike iD
DF: Odd
CO: UK
YP: 2007

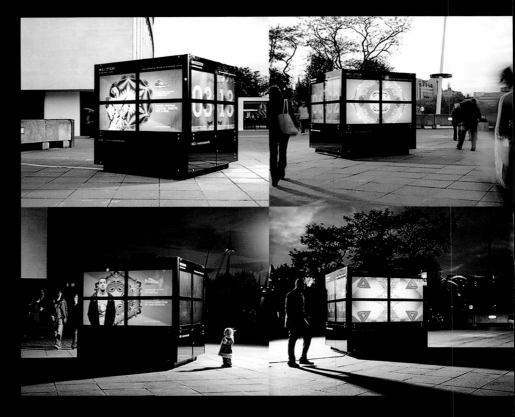

# Learn

hen the club Soho
ridge foreign languages
t your service. We
reak stereotypes in
ducation. Based on the
ommunicative approach,
e have developed a
ew basic programmes
 courses on English,
erman, Italian, French
nd Chinese.

L: Soho Bridge
E: Denis Dadaev
O: Ukrainez
P: 2007

Клуб иностранных
языков

# Change

Over the past two years the Oxfam 'Generation Why' sub-brand dramatically improved perceptions of Oxfam amongst people engaged in the youth programme. However, qualitative research into youth communications revealed a number of shortcomings. So, Oxfam commissioned ODD to develop a new communications strategy, identity and creative approach to their youth marketing.

The brief was to refresh Oxfam's youth identity to ensure that it appealed strongly to the target audience; adds value to Oxfam's brand rather than diluting it; competes favourably with communications from other brands in the same marketplace.

CL: Oxfam
DF: Odd
CO: UK
YP: 2007

C: Optimo & Strukto
D: CEMEX-
   DALMACIJACEMENT
T: TRIDVAJEDAN market
   communication Ltd
D: Izvorka Juric
D: Izvorka Juric
C: Izvorka Juric
D: Croatia

# Mooorro

The Workshop Vostok
went to Stockholm to
collect a prize which
was a Merit Award which
is like a very cool
but I do not drink and
led, and were also
taking a cocktail into
the hall of the Nobel
which is all gold and
bueníiisima gave a meal
and I here in Barcelona
eating frozen muffins
and the Siren of Litel.
The award is given by
the so-Get Up, is a
hairdresser and prestige
will not like that my
yaya that is old and
only have magazines
Talk Shows, finally ...
will be again.

---

TI: Get Up Printing Kit
CL: Get Up
DF: Alexis Rom estudio
DE: Alexis Rom
    Claude Marzotto
PH: Carlotta Broglia
CO: Spain
YP: 2008

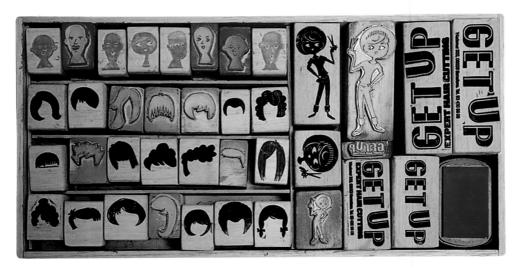

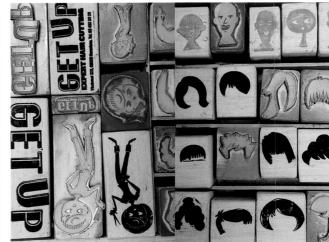

# Balloon

Dott is a ten year programme of design innovation, initiated by the Design Council, that will take place every two years in a different region or nation across the UK. The programme encourages the innovative use of design as contribution to economic, cultural and social success of the UK and will provide the opportunity for designers, businesses and public service providers to engage with citizens in improving national life through design.

Dott will be an inspiring, involving and educational initiative for young people and various groups of citizens. Its aim is to raise knowledge of the value and importance of design to our wellbeing. Each Dott biennial will respond to the specific needs and ambitons of the region concerned. The aim is to foster an inclusive and participatory approach to design that will stimulate long-term change and create a lasting legacy. Dott 07 will take eight core themes - energy and environment, sustainable tourism, school and community, health and wellbeing, mobility and access, town and country, food and nutrition, and housing and home - and work with local communities within the region to frame specific challenges as design opportunities.

CL: Dott
CO: UK
YP: 2007

# Underwear

Catriona MacKechnie, the Meatpacking District's luxe intimate apparel boutique, is offering lingerie, loungewear and swimwear from top designers, including Dolce & Gabbana, Chloé and ID Sarrieri.

---

CL: Catriona MacKechnie

# Shoes

ASCIS the name "ANIMA SAMA IN CORPORE SANO" acronym. After all these years, ASICS products experienced a lot of changes. In 1956 Melbourne Olympic Games in the preparatory process, ONITSUKA set ASCIS company's business philosophy: the most suitable for the development of sports products. In the 1967 Tokyo Olympics, dressed in brand shoes TIGER athletes won a total of 46 medals. By 1970, TIGER become the nation's largest running shoe manufacturers and 70 percent of the well-known athletes are wearing TIGER shoes.

TI: Onitsuka Tiger
CL: Asics
DF: MNP Design
YP: 2008

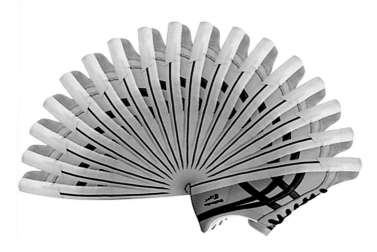

**MADE OF JAPAN**

**MADE OF JAPAN**

**MADE OF JAPAN**

# Billboard

The new Wieden +
Kennedy brand campaign
for the newspaper – The
Guardian.
Owned by no-one. Free
to say anything.

CI: Campaign
CL: The Guardian
YP: 2007

# Street

Bankside Mix advert at
bus stop.
Bankside Mix adverts on
upcoming shops.
Bankside Mix advert on
construction fence.
Bankside Mix — new
cafes and shops in the
Bankside area.
Bankside Mix advert on
construction fence.

TI: Bankside
YP: 2008

# Posters

180 Years of UCL
People.

---

CL: UCL
CO: UK

# Beautiful

TI: SWEET GARDEN
DF: Unitedidea
    Advertising
CD: Hisen
AD: Hisen
DE: Chen Yan
CO: China

# Home

TI: HEIRLOOM
DF: Unitedidea
    Advertising
CD: Hisen
AD: Hisen
DE: Hisen
CO: China

海南和阳实业有限公司
电话: 0898-66798111  66192111
地址: 海口市国贸大道48号新世界商务2303

# Beach

C: Century Beach
F: Unitedidea
   Advertising
D: Hisen
I: Hisen
C: Hisen
D: China

# Wind

TI: Graceful Humane
    Life
DF: Unitedidea
    Advertising
CD: Hisen
AD: Hisen
DE: Hisen
CO: China

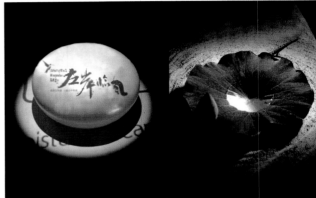

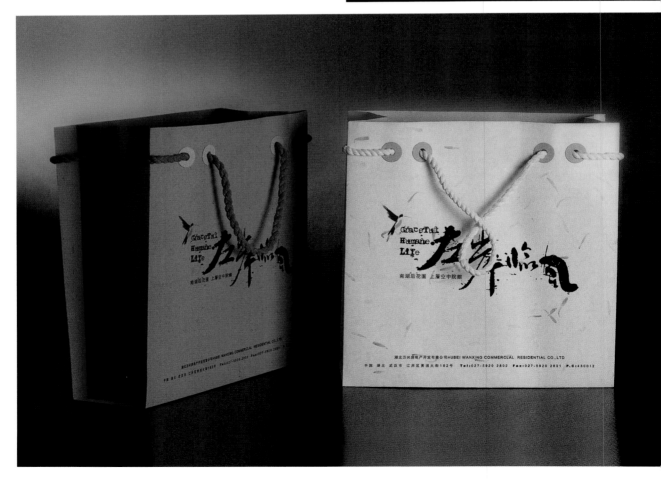

T: Top-grade Town
F: Unitedidea
   Advertising
D: Hisen
D: Hisen
E: He Wei
O: China

# Jewelry

This Jewelry design,
Stationery system.

---

CL: Decamp
DF: Public Design

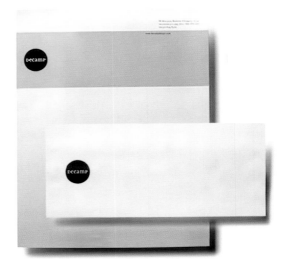

# Perm

Create an interactive business card that illustrates some of the services of the salon; the men's card shows a man's hair going from gray to brown and the women's card shows the woman's hair going from straight to curly. Creative Suitcase is an award-winning graphic design, advertising and Web design studio located in Austin, Texas. We have produced a wide variety of projects, including branding, logos, identity systems, brochures, Web sites and print campaigns for clients ranging from non-profits to Fortune 500 companies.

TI: Impact Salon
DE: Creative Suitcase

. French restaurant
nd bar.

1.

2.

# Brochure

Newspaper advert on 'The Times'. The Overture - a Southbank Centre celebration, which welcomes back the Royal Festival Hall after two years of restoration and redevelopment. Sorprediendonos again with these favorites of editorial design, a hug.

---

TI: Southbank Centre
YP: 2007

與500強爲鄰，開拓無限可能

New World Group is one of the ten consortiums and land agents in Hong Kong, which have 30 years' international the property management, capital construction, service, telecom. It's internal flagship of property --

NWTC
NEW WORLD TRADE CENTRE
新世界国贸大厦

新世界中国地产有限公司
New World China Land Limited

與500強爲鄰

New World Group is one of the ten consortiums and land agents in HongKong,which have 30 years' international the property management, capital construction,service,telecom. It's internal flagship of property --

NWTC
NEW WORLD TRADE CENTRE
新世界国贸大厦

新世界中国地产有限公司
New World China Land Limited

## Business

TI: New World Trade
    Centre
DF: RITO brand design
    and promotion
CO: China

**Forbes**

與500強爲鄰，
每天都有愉快的邀約

一次偶然的相遇，成了我們合作的開始

新世界國貿大廈

NWTC
新世界國貿大廈

新世界國貿大廈
NEW WORLD TRADE CENTRE

全球化商貿平台

新世界中國地產有限公司
New World China Land Limited

08:00　　18:00　　02:00

完善配套、便捷高效

NWTC
新世界國貿大廈

新世界中國地產有限公司
New World China Land Limited

新世界國貿大廈
金融街的黃金地段

NWTC
新世界國貿大廈

新世界中國地產有限公司
New World China Land Limited

新世界國貿大廈
全球化商貿樞紐

NWTC
新世界國貿大廈

新世界中國地產有限公司
New World China Land Limited

 86-027-85752721　85747929

實力見証品質　新世界集團發展兼管理逾100萬M²建設面積

NWTC
新世界國貿大廈

新世界中國地產有限公司
New World China Land Limited

# Glass

Bring your heart token
with you on the night.

TI: Heart
YP: 2008

# heart

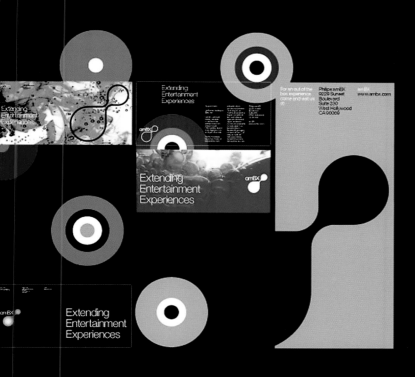

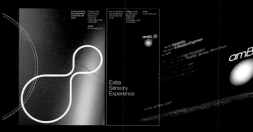

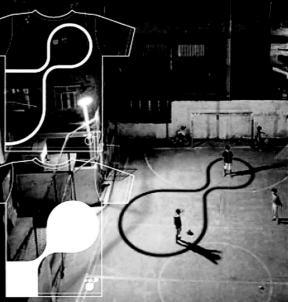

# Match

This is the Primal Restraurant of Company Identity.

---

TI: Laguna Beach CA
CL: Primal Restraurant
YP: 2008

# Logo

These logo are nice,
but the presentation/
pictures make them even
nicer... Beautiful logo
design work.

I: Southbank Centre
F: Stylestation
E: Jan Finnesand

# Printing

Special thanks to wim crouwel for granting us permission to reproduce this poster and for consulting with us to make this possible. The poster has been meticulously restored from the original, making it an exact replica of the 1968 version drawn by wim crouwels own hand. The poster will be reprinted in an edition of 250 units. Reprint of the 1968 original stedelijk museum poster, produced in association with wim crouwel, 2008. Image detail - double checking against pantone black to measure density of black ink on proof with the consistency of the 1968 original version. the camera hasn't picked this up tonally or its not noticeable but the black of the lower print it too dense to match the original so this print is scrapped.

TI: Reprint
YP: 2008

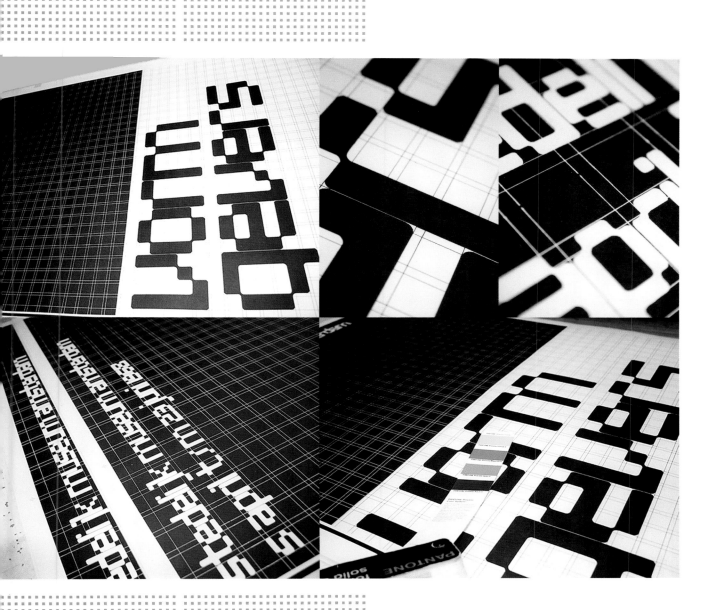

# Letter

This "letter field" is located right next to the Berlin gallery and was designed by Kuhn Malvezzi in 2003/04.
It's probably 100 yards long and consists of 160 letters of famous and not so famous artists whose works were or are still exposed in the Berlin gallery.
Standing in the middle of the letter field it gets kinda dadaistic cause it's very hard to read any name at all - all you see is just letters.
For example you will only be able to read the name "Nussbaum" at the lower right half of my photo.

TI: an old one from the tour w / patstome

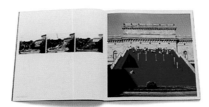

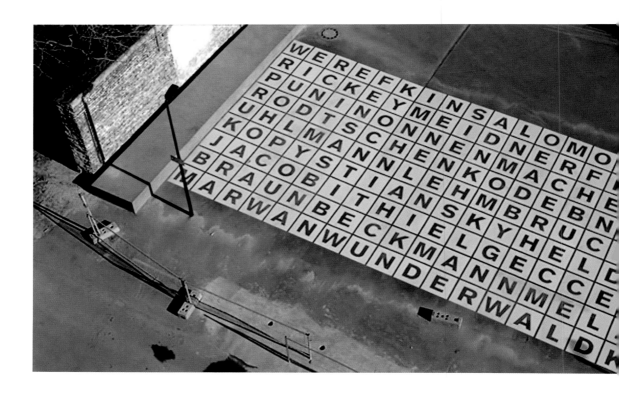

# Film

The 57th Berlin Film
Festival's competition
line-up (which, as
usual, strangely
includes a handful of
films that are not in
competition) represents
most continents, though
English-language
productions dominate
the list of 26 motion
pictures. Among these
are 19 world premieres,
six international
premieres, and one
European premiere.
Twenty-two of the
shortlisted films are
competing for the
Golden Bear.

---

I: Berlin Film Festival
   2007 Film Line-Up
O: Germany
P: 2007

# Museum

TI: On Sculpture
DF: Doublestandards
    Studio
CO: Germany

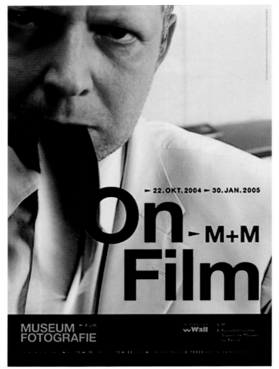

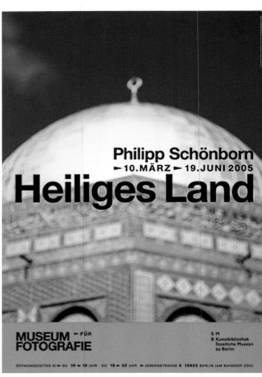

**Raimund Kummer**
**On**
➤ **25. JUNI** ➤ **26. SEPT. 2004**
**Sculpture**

**MUSEUM** ➤ FÜR
**FOTOGRAFIE**

MEDIENPARTNER
**Wall**

S M
B Kunstbibliothek
Staatliche Museen
zu Berlin

ÖFFNUNGSZEITEN DI ➤ SO **10** ➤ **18** UHR   DO **10** ➤ **22** UHR   ➤ JEBENSSTRASSE **2**  **10623** BERLIN (AM BAHNHOF ZOO)

# Culture

Broadway Greenwich
Village El Barrio.

CL: Haus Der Kulturen
    Der Welt
DF: Doublestandards
    Studio
CO: Germany
YP: 2007

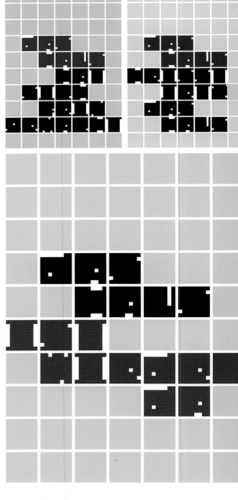

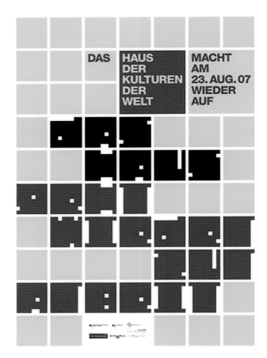

DAS HAUS DER KULTUREN DER WELT MACHT AM 23. AUG. 07 WIEDER AUF

DAS HAUS DER KULTUREN DER WELT MACHT AM 23. AUG. 07 WIEDER AUF

HAUS
DER
KULTUREN
DER
WELT

23.08. BIS 04.11.2007

DAS FEST
**72 Stunden
Non Stop**

MUSIK
**Broadway
Greenwich Village
El Barrio**

LITERATUR
**Dowtown
Uptown
Crosstown**

VORTRÄGE UND DISKUSSIONEN
**Transatlantische Gespräche**

AUSSTELLUNG UND FILME
**New York – States of Mind**

ASIEN-PAZIFIK-
WOCHEN
**usAsia**

# Skull

the public theater in
new york have placed
these ads all over the
subway and buses and
other places in the
city and for that i am
very glad. obviously a
great concept with the
ornamental hair on the
skull and a dandy bit
of execution too.

———————————————

TI: shakespeare in the
    park
YP: 2008

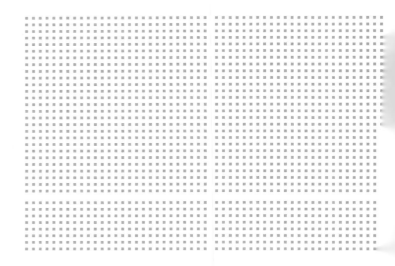

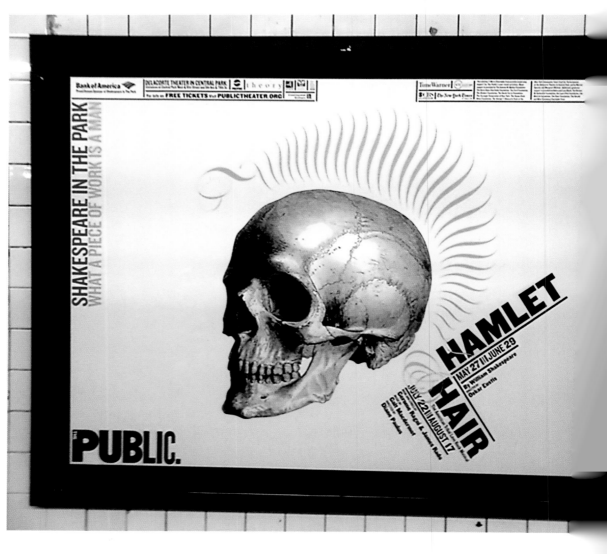

# Competition

Spielzeitbeginn Am
31.10.
Hebbel Am Ufer.

---

C: HAU
F: Doublestandards
   Studio
O: Germany
P: 2007

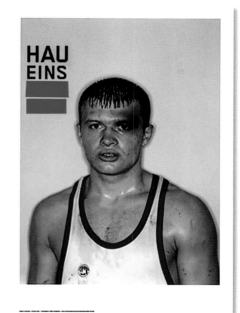

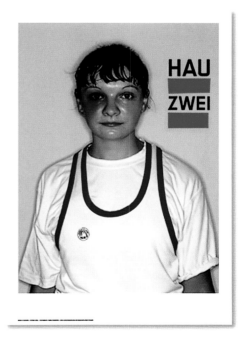

# Box

You can not imagine
the Doublestandards
studios have the
power and potential
of their diversified
development, the design
is very wide in various
fields have their own
possession. There are
specific binding books,
advertisements, posters,
display design, and
many other fine works,
with many well-known
global manufacturers
have.

---

TI: Auktion
DF: Doublestandards
    Studio
CO: Germany
YP: 2007

Tea

MadeThought Britain is
an integrated design
team, including many in
the field of design,
including products,
printing and so on, his
work is very modern and
simple generosity.

I: Yauatcha Packaging
F: MadeThought
o: UK
P: 2007

# Shadow

Some well-known world-class designers, has its own SELECT SHOP. Every year, many of them from the goods, a selection of classic top, and made available to those who pay attention to quality of life of people.

A SELECT, learn Chinese and foreign construction concept combines the essence of architecture, from the human point of view, to create the perfect landmark building.

CI is the design of a variety of factors together, we adhere to the principle of such a design. First: to highlight the internationalization of the product, quality of nobility; the second: the wisdom of life to the concept of communication with the public to explain the truth of life and the life. Third: contains a sense of cultural and aesthetic value. Fourth: consumer psychology, for the hearts and minds.

---

TI: A. SELECT
DF: SHAN YU YANG YANG
CD: Lai ZhaoYuan
AD: Lai ZhaoYuan
DE: Wang AnJian
    Gu Lei

KASHIWA SATO 1965 in Tokyo, was born in 1989 from Tama Art University graduate, and then for Hakuhodo Inc. Advertising agency, until 2000 to set up a "SAMURAI" workshop. He engaged in all aspects of the creative director and art, including product development, design and advertising space, and so on. He was a Japanese band SMAP publicity, advertising art director, as well as the Honda ads, GOKUNAMA Kirin beer ads, TSUTAYA creative director and so on and so on. Awards include: Tokyo ADC Award, Gold TDC Tokyo, Japan Association of Graphic Designer Award for young designers, the Asahi Award advertisements, Yusaku Kamekura prize package and Japan, such as the Gold Award for design.

———————————————

CL: SMAP
DE: KASHIWA SATO
CO: Japan

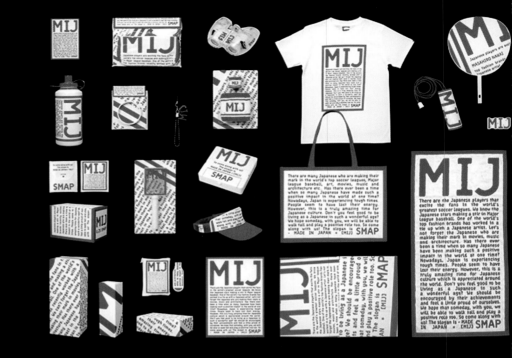

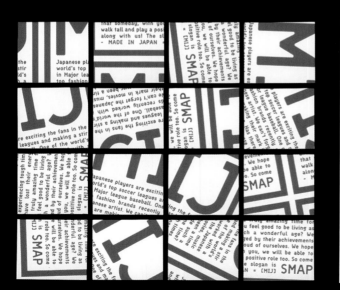

MIJ

there are the Japanese players that excite the fans in the world's greatest soccer leagues. We know the Japanese stars making a stir in Major league baseball. One of the world's top fashion brands has worked in a tie up with a Japanese artist. Let's not forget the Japanese who are making their mark in movies, music and architecture. Has there ever been a time when so many Japanese have been making such a positive impact in the world at one time? Nowadays, Japan is experiencing tough times. People seem to have lost their energy. However, this is a truly amazing time for Japanese culture which is appreciated around the world. Don't you feel good to be living as a Japanese in such a wonderful age? We should be encouraged by their achievements and feel a little proud of ourselves. We hope that someday, with you, we will be able to walk tall and play a positive role too. So come along with us! the slogan is
- MADE IN JAPAN = [MIJ] 6.25 SMAP

MIJ

There are many Japanese who are making their mark in the world's top soccer leagues, Major league baseball, art, movies, music and architecture etc.. Has there ever been a time when so many Japanese have made such a positive impact in the world at one time? Nowadays, Japan is experiencing tough times. People seem to have lost their energy. However, this is a truly amazing time for Japanese culture. Don't you feel good to be living as a Japanese in such a wonderful age? We hope someday, with you, we will be able to walk tall and play a positive role too. So come along with us! The slogan is MADE IN JAPAN = [MIJ] 6.25 SMAP

MIJ

We all know the Japanese who are fantasistas. In Major League is Japanese. There is the animated feature film. One of the world's top fashion worldwide

have play

time for Japanese culture. Don't you feel good to be living as a Japanese in such a wonderful age? We hope that someday, with you, we will be able to

ourselves.

# Coffee

Sundance Gourmet Coffee Co. takes Cape Town's coffee culture to a new level with its unique blend of vibey atmosphere, chic design and your favourite aromatic roast. Located in the heart of the city in Church and Buitengracht Streets as well as Mouille Point, Sundance Gourmet Coffee Co. offers the ultimate indulgence with an array of tempting cakes and chocolates, architecturally designed gourmet sandwiches and, of course, its coffee (which will excite the palate of any discerning java junkie). Free deliveries are made within the proximity of all three stores.

CL: Sundance Gourmet
    Coffee Shop
DF: Apartment Studios
CO: South Africa

# Ink

VINSEUM, el Museu de
la Cultures del Vi de
Catalunya ha convidat
l'escola a participar en
el programa Presències
a Palau que s'emet a
TVINSEUM.

CL: VINSEUM, Museu de
    les Cultures del Vi
    de
DF: Estudio Diego
    Feijóo
DE: Diego Feijóo
CO: Spain
YP: 2008

Museu de les Cultures del Vi de Catalunya

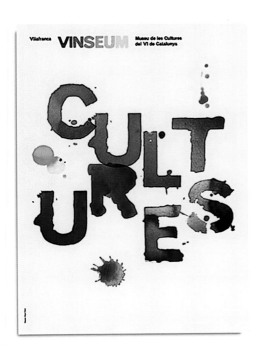

# Booklet

Corporate & Brand
Identity - ELI.

CL: ELI
YP: 2007

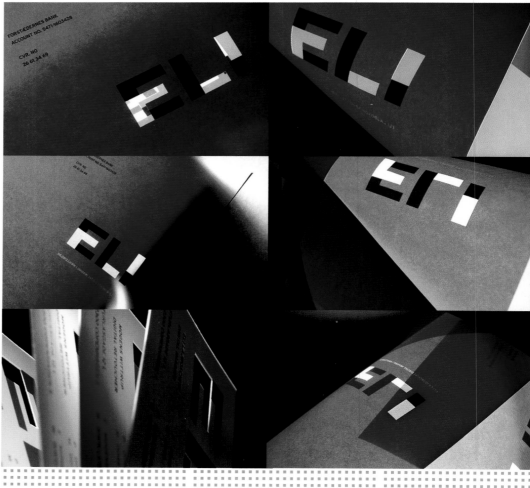

CL: Y Faith community
DF: UP & UP Design
CD: Yu XueHua
AD: Wu YuZhe
DE: Wu YuZhe
CO: China

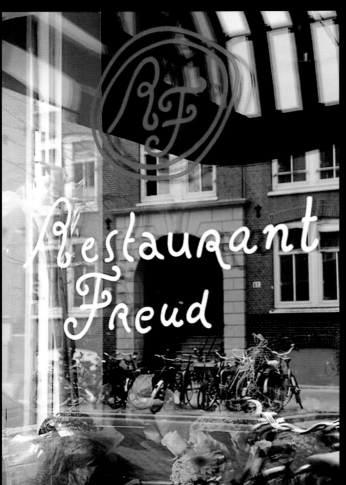

# Restaurant

Culinair is Restaurant
Freud: er wordt
gewerkt met zoveel
mogelijk biologische
ingrediënten,
seizoensgebonden. Maar
ook andere producten,
zoals koffie en thee,
worden met zorg gekozen;
volgens criteria
die goed zijn voor
samenleving en milieu.

CL: Restaurant Freud
DF: UbachsWisbrun/JWT
AD: Wim Ubachs
    Gerard Foekema
DE: Sake van den Brule
    Elke Kunneman
    Robin Winters
CO: Netherlands
YP: 2008

# Exhibition

Image design for a piercing of the hole, is a breakthrough from the inside out by watching the outside, but also represent the individual's sense of calling.

TI: A Discrimination Art & Design Exhibition
DF: Dragon Doing Communications
DE: Bao Bin
CO: China

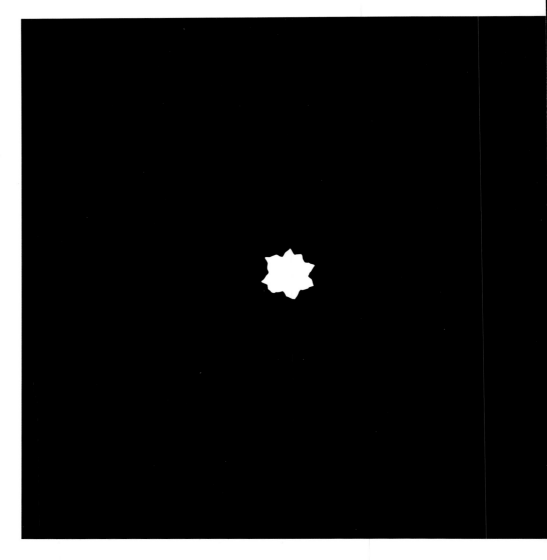

1個歧視
藝術設計邀請展
A DISCRIMINATION
ART&DESIGN EXHIBITION

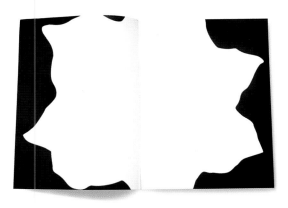

# Reading

Get London Reading is a campaign by Booktrust to get Londoners reading books set in London. To promote the campaign, KentLyons have created a selection of installations around London, showing extracts from books in situ.
The extracts appear on pavements, windows and rubbish, as though the words have fallen from a book.
Installations in and around the Truman Brewery on Brick Lane. The quote is from Brick Lane, by Monica Ali.
Box installations for Get London Reading. Sprayed with a variety of water-based inks.
The laser-cut stencils for the Get London Reading installation. Laser-cut out of linseed oil covered paper.
Get London Reading Installations on Mill Street, featuring a quote from Oliver Twist by Charles Dickens.

---

TI: Get London Reading
CO: UK
YP: 2008

A stranger, looking from one of the wooden bridges thrown across it at Mill Lane, will see the inhabitants of the houses on either side lowering from their back doors and windows, buckets, pails, domestic utensils of all kinds, in which to haul the water up;

Oliver Twist by Charles Dickens

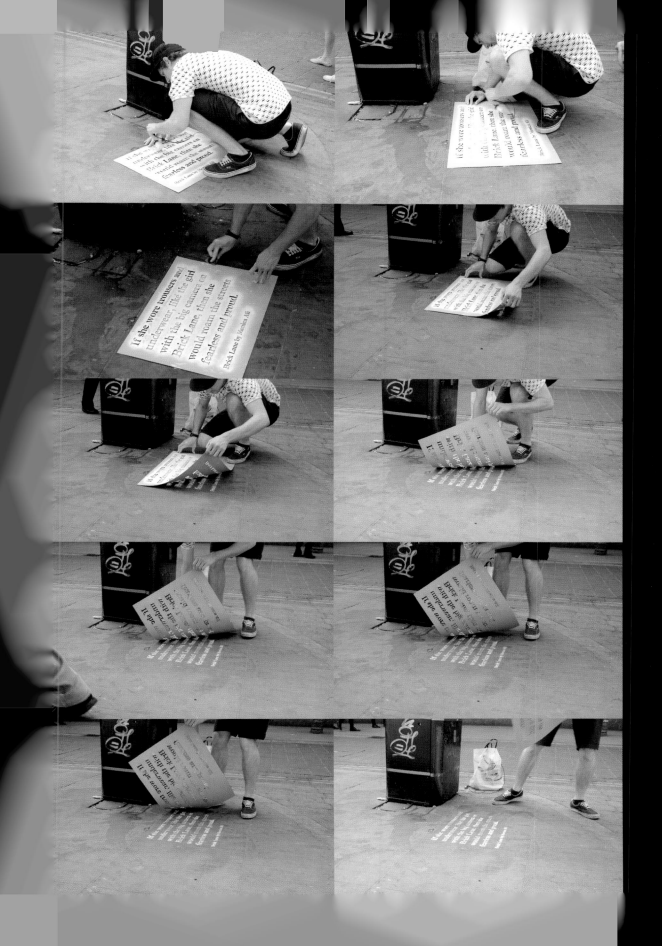

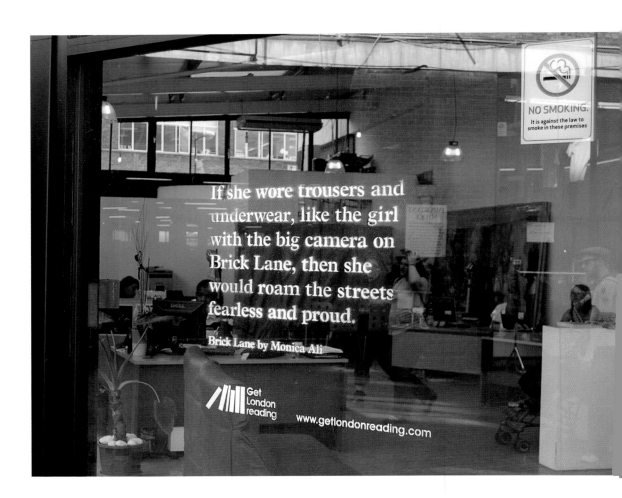

# Cosmetics

Sumptuous packaging for the Thymes 'Kimono Rose' line of fragrances and soaps. This work is featured in the American Institute of Graphic Artists Design Archives. Brad Surcey was the primary designer and I worked at Duffy on the technical and 3D aspects of the package design.

---

TI: Thymes Kimono Rose
    Packaging
CO: USA
YP: 2008

# Love

The Aerial Army of Love, a collective of Seattle's own professional and amateur aerialists dedicated to helping world relief organizations through aerial performance, is throwing their third annual aerial benefit this April. The benefit, AerLift III, is a one-night event showcasing a variety of aerial arts including aerial hoop, silks, corde lisse, and various forms of trapeze. Performers include members of Circus Contraption, the Aerialistas, the Cabiri, Little Red Studio, the School of Acrobatics and New Circus Arts (SANCA), Kirkland Dance Center, and many students taught by local aerialist and Aerial Army of Love founder Lara Paxton.

TI: Aerlift
CO: USA
YP: 2008

## poster

Oloom is a group of
designers involved in
interior design and
architecture. The
poster, screen printed
on different stock of
paper, was also cut
into letterheads and
business cards.

TI: Oloom visual
    identity

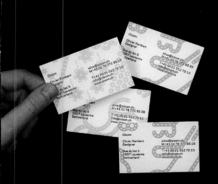

# Octopus

The name 'Area 17' refers to the optical cortex of the brain where vision is processed. It also refers to our interactive agency where vision is realized.

CL: nove
DF: Area17
CO: France
YP: 2008

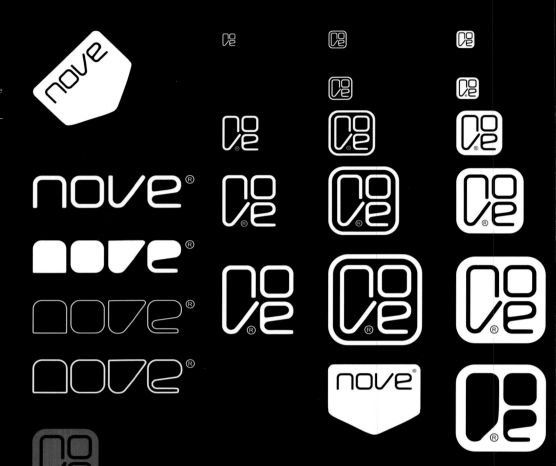

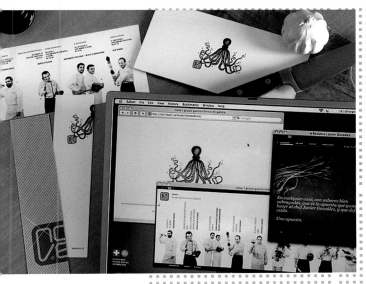

# Horse

Branding and interior
design for Grand, a new
home, furnishings store
in Somerville, MA.

_____

TI: Grand

# Impression

TI: MA BANG
CD: Wang Song
AD: Wang Song
DE: Wang Song
CO: China
YP: 2007

By Felix Ng
www.silnt.com

# Herbs

This special jumbo
issue, curated by Steve
Lawler (mojoko) invited
40 international artists
to contribute based on
the theme, Health.
Our contribution is
based on the old wife's
saying - "Remember to
drink soup" featuring
traditional Chinese
herbs.

TI: Artwork for Fl.ag
    issue 15
DE: Felix Ng
YP: 2008

# Bracket

Bracket is a publication that features everything-in-between - ideas, process and voices overlooked and under-appreciated. The business card we designed, looks deceivingly empty until pushed open to reveal a bracket that frames the information.

TI: Business Card
DE: Felix Ng
YP: 2008

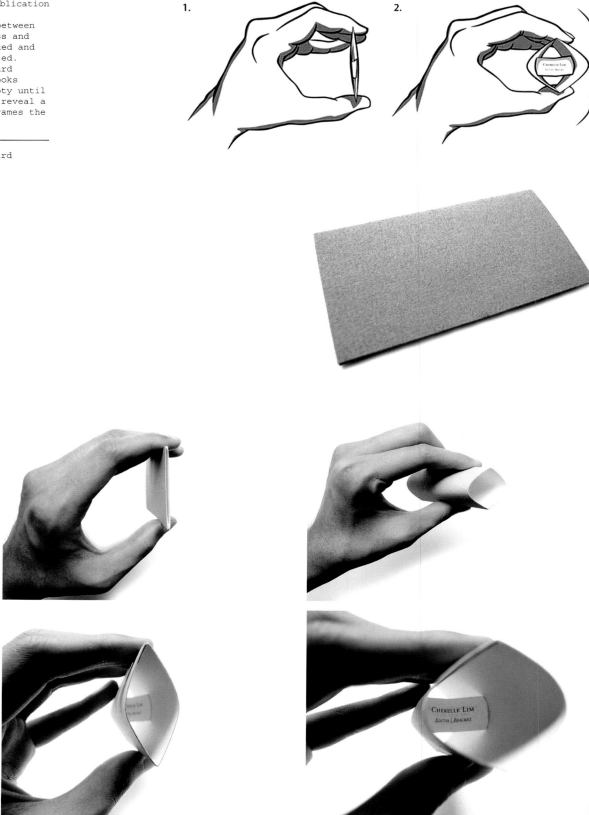

Cover

The cover of this programme is a folded poster stapled to the booklet. 125 × 176 mm stapled brochure. Once unfolded, the poster shows a chaotic heap of typography. Only when you start flipping through the pages do the illustrations start to make sense.

TI: Theater program
    Vevey
YP: 2007

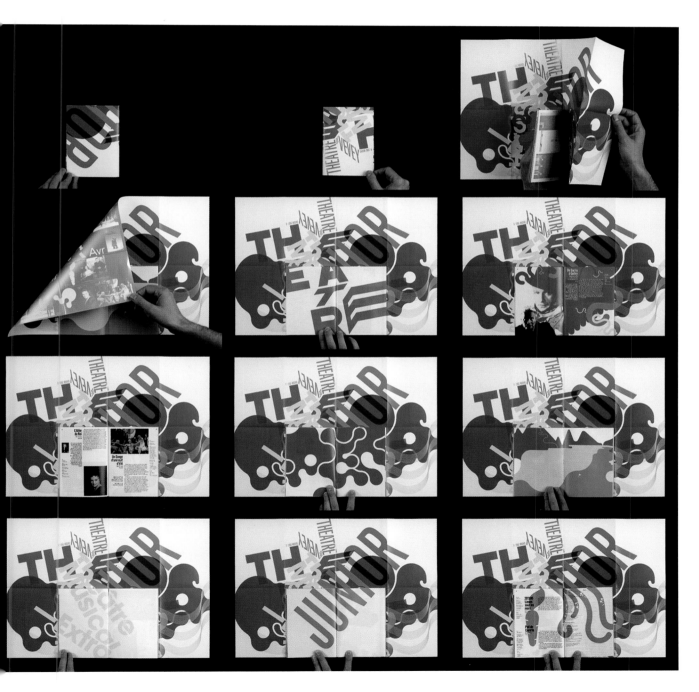

# Music

Identity system
"Boy Alexander" for
Alexander Chen a.k.a.
Boy in Static (musical
activities) a.k.a.
Carbonated Jazz (art &
design).

CL: Boy Alexander
YP: 2008

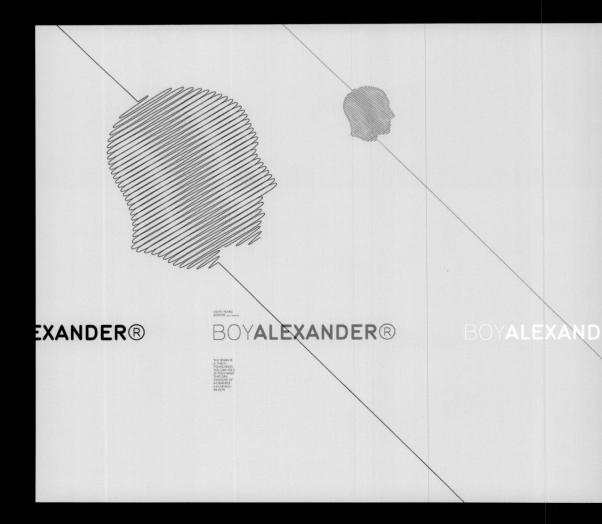

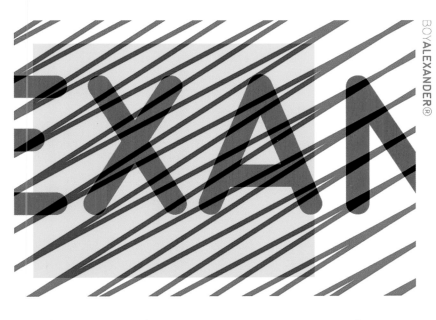

 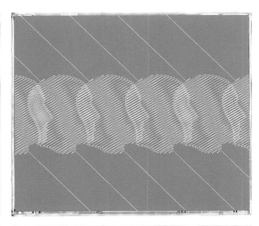

# Health

The foundation of the
Immuno-Viva product
line, Core's wide range
of health benefits are
nearly unsurpassed.
Loaded with synergistic
antioxidants and Omega
3s and 6s, It powerfully
supports cardiovascular
health, immune function,
and proper inflammation
response.

TI: Immuno-Viva Core
YP: 2008

# Wine

Every Christmas it
seems, Duffy & Partners
send a bottle of wine
to clients and friends,
each year a different
set of designs, some
lovely thoughts (I love
the ba humbug one!).
Here is a selection
over the years...

TI: Happy Holidays
DF: Duffy & Partners
YP: 2008

HAPPY
HOLIDAYS

# Umbrella

And grabbed the lead in
cutting-edge, folding
umbrella from the figure
reveals. Looks like a
bottle of hardcover as
well as fun.
As a gift unique design
is also recommended.
TSUTONKARA a beautiful,
simple design.
And open the bottle,
there is a hidden
folding umbrella!
Location is slim to
TORAZU bottle, feel
free to always keep
in your bag you can
remember. Bottle of
the hardcover are in a
hurry because the train
with an umbrella to
fold up when I run.

TI: Folding umbrella
CO: Japan
YP: 2008

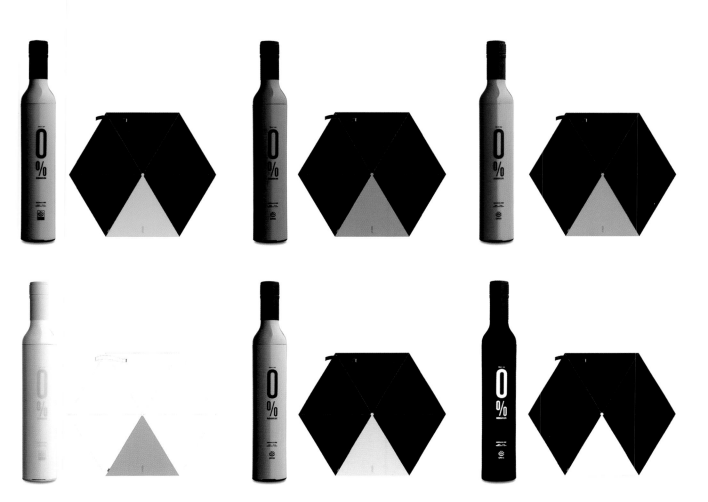

# Collection

Using the everyday
graphic language of
symbols, we created
this A1 poster.
Screen-printed in
phosphorescent ink by
K2 Screen.
Screenprinted with glow
in the dark ink on gf
smith 175 gsm dark
grey colorplan. This
poster was the first
in a series specially
commissioned, limited
edition print and
available exclusively
to blanka.

---

TI: Symbolism
CO: UK

'Symbolism'
By Build, for Blanka 01/06
Edition of 100 only

# Face

A set of 3 triptych's
(Growth/Cycle/Cycle)
& a single poster
(Nurture/Nature),
commissioned by +81
magazine (Japan). Under
the theme/title 'Think
Global, Act Local', the
posters were displayed
in a selection of The
North Face shops in
Japan.

TI: THE NORTH FACE
CO: Japan
YP: 2008

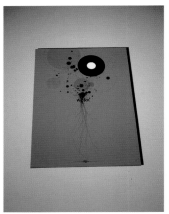

# Wall

This advertising
2008 typography.
Exhibitions-and-
installations identity-
and-branding.
Identity and exhibition
design for the Getty
Images Advertising
Activism at Cannes Lions
08 events. Collateral
includes flyers/press/
outdoor exhibition &
signage.

TI: Advertising Activism
CO: France
YP: 2008

# Black

Icon set design for
the 2007 D&AD Global
Awards. Commissioned
by Saatchi & Saatchi
[London]. Taking the
simple D&AD hexagon,
but approaching it in a
3d & 2d way we produced
this set of simple
icons. Produced by This
is Real Art.
View the D&AD 'Global
Awards 2007 Nominations
exhibition' postcard
set here.

TI: D&AD ICON SET
CO: UK
YP: 2007

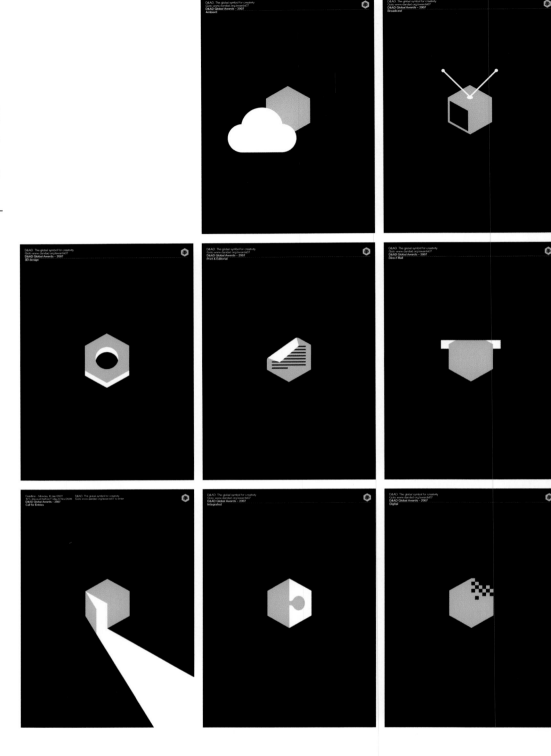

D&AD. The global symbol for creativity
Goto www.dandad.org/awards07
**D&AD Global Awards – 2007**
**Branding**

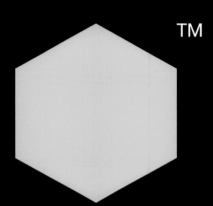

TM

# Black

8x A5 postcard set
[+ A3 folded poster]
enclosed in a custom
foil blocked slip case.
Forms part of the print
communication of the
D&AD 'Global Nominations
Awards exhibition 2007'.
Under the title 'Ideas
are Fragile' we applied
the Global Awards icons
[also designed by us
commissioned by Saatchi
& Saatchi, London] to
sheets of glass, which
were then dropped and
photographed shattering
at high speed by Jason
Tozer.

TI: D&AD ICON SET
CO: UK

# Label

Compact disc sleeve
design for the Sun
Electric release 'Lost
& Found' on the Shit
Katapult label. Sleeve
includes a custom
typeface design (B-THN).

---

TI: SUN ELECTRIC - LOST
& FOUND
CO: Germany
YP: 2008

# Packaging

Compact disc sleeve design for the inaugral release of Record Camp, a Brooklyn based electronic music label. The compilation Brooklyn Keeps on Takin it comes packaged in a reverse board slipcase, with a reversible cover (photography by Adesh). Logo also designed by Build.

I: BROOKLYN KEEPS ON TAKIN' IT
O: UK

*Brooklyn Keeps on Takin' it.

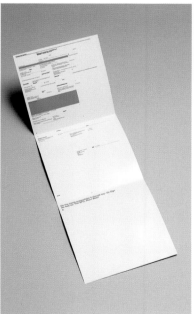

— *Trademark symbol*
— *AUS Records 12"/300° Generic sleeve.*
*Knowledge is power — www.ausmusic.co.uk / info@ausmusic.co.uk /aus logo by Build.*

# Record

Label identity / 12"
Record sleeve & labels.
House-bag design with
cut-out label view
[on the reverse]. Logo
design/identity & print
collateral including
online ads. Aus is the
sister label of Simple
records.

---

TI: AUS RECORDS
CO: UK

Sideshow
— *'Scary Biscuits EP'*
(AUS0601)

—827170 11796 9
—TM

— *Trademark symbol*
— *AUS Records 12"/300° Generic sleeve.*
*Knowledge is power — www.ausmusic.co.uk / info@ausmusic.co.uk /Aus logo by Build.*

—AUS0601
— Recorded, engineered and produced by Sideshow.
— Executive producer
Published by Simple Music publishing ltd.
© 2006 by the Simple Publishing ltd.
Distributed by Kudos and Renaissance 1td.. Mastering by Shane/Heathmans.
www.livetransitsound.net

Side 1 (over)—
1 — *Polar Bear Dub* (33rpm)
2 — *Scary Biscuits* (33rpm)
3 — *You've Changed Dub* (33rpm)
Side 2 (here)—
1 — *Scary Biscuits (John Tejada Remix)* (45rpm)

# Simple

label identity / 12"
record sleeve & labels
utilising the distinct
strikethrough branding.
housebag & label design
with cut-out label view
printed on reverse
board. Logo & all print
collateral including
online advertising.
simple records is the
sister label of Aus.

I: SIMPLE RECORDS -
   HOUSEBAG
O: UK

# Product

Dead Format series shirts for 2K/Gingham. Celebrating the demise of popular formats that we grew up and loved. Featuring- Audio Cassette/Floppy Diskette & VHS cassette. Rest in peace.

---

TI: DEAD FORMATS
CO: UK

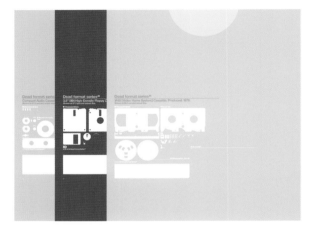

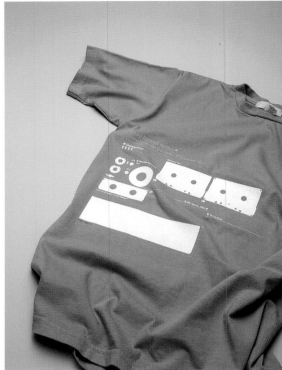

# Time'code"

## Product

Self initiated project,
time'code" series of
shirts. Celebrating
some of our favourite
songs in minutes &
seconds. Produced and
available to buy from
Blanka.

TI: TIME CODE SERIES
CO: UK

# Shop

Logo & branding for
The Design Museum Shop
(London), designed to
re-launch the online
store and refresh
the branding of the
physical shop within
the museum itself.
Collateral includes,
in-store signage,
printed brochure & re-
usable shopping-bag.

TI: DESIGN MUSEUM SHOP
CO: UK
YP: 2007

# FREE RE-USABLE BAG WITH EVERY PURCHASE OVER £25! OR BUY ONE FOR JUST £1!

# Brand

Pottery Barn Kids products are kid-sized versions of grown-up favorites sold by Pottery Barn, some are inspired by classic American childhood themes. Using this as inspiration, Character designed a branding system, which includes business cards, stationery system and collateral. Character created over twenty original icons illustrating children interacting with products in a playful way.

---

CL: Pottery Barn Kids
DF: Character design
CD: Patricia
     Tish Evangelista
     Rishi Shourie
     Ben Pham
AD: Lian Ng
DE: Eugene Chung
     Lora Tomova
     Andrew Johnson

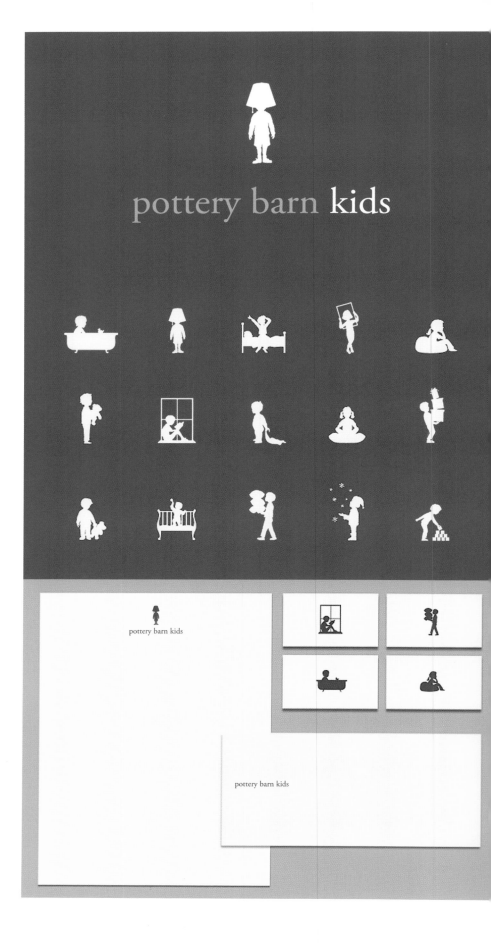

# pottery barn kids

## spring sprouts

The most playful time of the year is here. Just as the robins move to watch for worms, so we see our children become more active. The babies ever begin to crawl or walk, and the older ones start to recognize the cycles in life. Questions of who, what and why fill the air, so we encourage you to keep the answers handy and the climate warm. Our pieces for playing, thinking and resting create just the right atmosphere. It's a collection designed to nurture their inquisitive minds, and help them grow.

## sunshine

An inexhaustible appreciation of childhood lies at the heart of kids. Our collection captures the playfulness of youth and is a warming and imaginative point for bedrooms, play rooms, and every room beyond. The collection also follows the Pottery Barn you know and love, with comfort, style, casual and relaxed. From pajamas to PJs pajamas, these decorations will keep your kids' spirits while also enriching your dreams for your very own days and nights. Enjoy.

# Brand

Character partnered with Pottery Barn Kids in 1999 to design the fledgling company's brand identity. The collaboration then extended to development and art direction of the Pottery Barn Kid's catalog, as well as design of retail system, in-store packaging, hang tags, shopping bags and gift registry collateral.
After the enormously successful launch of the catalog, Pottery Barn Kid's next step was to open retail stores. Character partnered with the retail division of Pottery Barn Kids to develop and design the in-store system, including signage, packaging, hang tags, shopping bags and gift registry collateral.

CL: Pottery Barn Kids
DF: Character design
CD: Patricia
    Tish Evangelista
    Rishi Shourie
    Ben Pham
AD: Lian Ng
DE: Eugene Chung
    Lora Tomova
    Andrew Johnson

# Tag

Tag designs for Japanese
paper company Takeo. 3
tags for actual objects
- Tape Measure/Colour
Pencil/Compass. 3 tags
for 'conceptual' items
- Empty Salbutamol
Inhaler/Paperclip/
Floppy Disc.

TI: TAKEO PAPER SHOW
CO: Japan

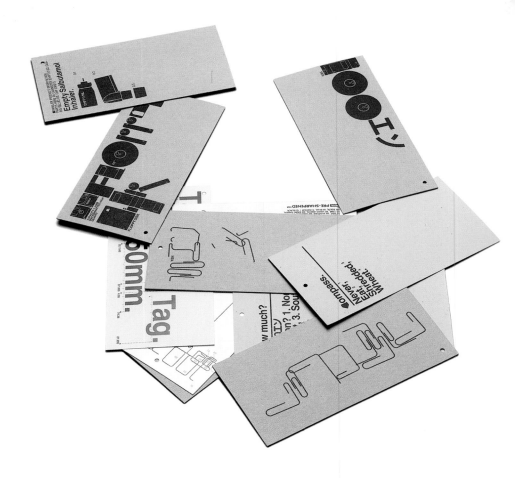

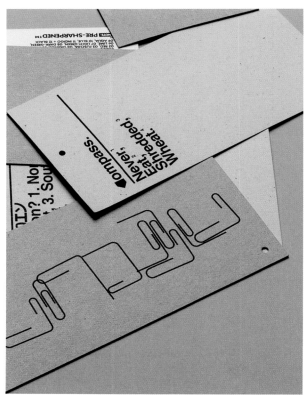

How much?
▶100エン
Pardon? 1. North,
2. East, 3. South,
4. West.

◀Compass.
Never,¹
Eat,²
Shredded,³
Wheat.⁴

Empty Salbutamol
Inhaler.

Tape
Measure* Tag.
100x50mm.

*Length: 5 Metre or 5000 Millimetres.
Complete with Carry strap™

100エン
Figure + Kata-
kana.

Price: 100 Yen.
42pt Helvetica Bold Type.
4.25pt Helvetica Bold Type.

FLOPPY DISK

Empty/Nil.

# Culture

C focuses on all aspects of art and culture, for large and small audiences. The organisation needs to campaign for subscribers in order to operate within the public domain of broadcasting. Studio Dumbar created the name C as well as the colourful, multilayered logo and a range of variants.

---

TI: Visual identity of C, broadcasting organisation
CL: C, broadcasting organisation for art and culture
DF: Studio Dumbar
CD: Michel de Boer
AD: Vincent van Baar
CO: Netherlands
YP: 2008

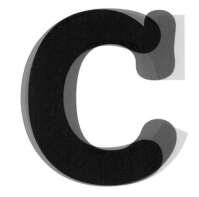

omroep voor kunst en cultuur

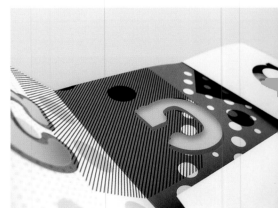

## C nieuws

**Billy Henderson van de Spinners overleden**
*04-02-2007*
In de Amerikaanse staat Florida is vrijdag zanger Billy Henderson...

**Martin Scorsese krijgt prijs Directors Guild of America**
*04-02-2007*
Martin Scorsese lijkt eindelijk kans te maken...

**Toneelhistoricus Ben Albach overleden**
*03-02-2007*
Toneelhistoricus en recensent Ben Albach...

**Amarins Wierdsma wint Davina van Wely vioolconcours**
*03-02-2007*
De 15-jarige Amarins Wierdsma is de winnares...

**Schrijfster Patricia de Martelaere ontbreekt in literatuurgeschiedenis**
*03-02-2007*
In de grote, uitpuilende literatuurgeschiedenis...

**Conflict tussen erfgenamen Goudstikker en advocaat**
*02-02-2007*
De restitutie van schilderijen uit de collectie van kunsthandelaar...

**Tiger Awards en nog veel meer prijzen uitgereikt in Rotterdam**
*02-02-2007*
De films Love Conquers All van Tan Chui Mui...

**Israel Museum moet kunstwerken teruggeven**
*02-02-2007*
De Israëlische regering heeft het Israël Museum...

Pagina 1 van 5 pagina('s) 1 | 2 | 3 > Laatste »

© C - omroep voor kunst en cultuur 2006 Pers | Contact | Disclaimer en privacyverklaring

---

**omroep voor kunst en cultuur**

→ Word lid!
→ C nieuws
→ Nu op C
→ Over C
→ Links

→ C gids
→ C agenda

Zoek

---

## Nu op C

Web-TV   Web-radio

RSS

Selecteer op [ datum ▾ ]

Playing                    0:07/59:59

### Rize
### David laChapelle
*2005 - 90 min*

**Programma titel**
Lorem ipsum dolor sit amet, consectetuer adipiscing.

**Lorem ipsum dolor sit amet**
Lorem ipsum dolor sit amet, consectetuer adipiscing elit.

**Lorem ipsum**
Lorem ipsum dolor sit amet, consectetuer adipiscing.

**Lorem ipsum**
Lorem ipsum dolor sit amet, consectetuer adipiscing. Aliquam venenatis quam vitae.

**Programma titel**
Lorem ipsum dolor sit amet, consectetuer adipiscing.

Lorem ipsum dolor sit amet, consectetuer adipiscing elit. Aliquam venenatis quam vitae magna. Lorem ipsum dolor sit amet, consectetuer adipiscing elit. Cras quis nibh ac ipsum gravida pulvinar. Aenean est quam, malesuada ut, congue vitae, dictum eget, nibh.

Etiam ligula arcu, nonummy sed, tincidunt a, bibendum nec, orci. Pellentesque ornare lacinia turpis. Proin lobortis. Nulla ac ipsum. Integer laoreet aliquam purus. Ut velit. Fusce ultrices, arcu eu pharetra rutrum, urna ipsum tincidunt leo, non ullamcorper eros erat vel tortor. Mauris condimentum aliquam leo.

---

**C**
**omroep voor kunst en cultuur**

→ Word lid!
→ C nieuws
→ Nu op C
→ Over C
→ Links

→ C gids
→ C agenda

Zoek

---

## C kunst en cultuur agenda

◄ augustus ►                    RSS

| ma | di | wo | do | vr | za | zo |
|----|----|----|----|----|----|----|
| 30 | 31 | 1  | 2  | 3  | 4  | 5  |
| 6  | 7  | 8  | 9  | 10 | 11 | 12 |
| 13 | 14 | 15 | 16 | 17 | 18 | 19 |
| 20 | 21 | 22 | 23 | 24 | 25 | 26 |
| 27 | 28 | 29 | 30 | 31 | 1  | 2  |

**dinsdag 22 augustus**

**Lorem ipsum**
*Locatie 21-08-2006 t/m 21-09-2006*
Lorem ipsum dolor sit amet, consectetuer adipiscing elit. Vivamus orci nibh, accumsan sodales, ullamcorper eu, feugiat non, enim.

**Lorem ipsum**
*Locatie 21-08-2006 t/m 21-09-2006*
Lorem ipsum dolor sit amet, consectetuer adipiscing elit. Vivamus orci nibh, accumsan sodales, ullamcorper eu, feugiat non, enim.

**Lorem ipsum**
*Locatie 21-08-2006 t/m 21-09-2006*
Lorem ipsum dolor sit amet, consectetuer adipiscing elit. Vivamus orci nibh, accumsan sodales, ullamcorper eu, feugiat non, enim.

**Lorem ipsum**
*Locatie 21-08-2006 t/m 21-09-2006*
Lorem ipsum dolor sit amet, consectetuer adipiscing elit. Vivamus orci nibh, accumsan sodales, ullamcorper eu, feugiat non, enim.

---

**C**
**omroep voor kunst en cultuur**

→ Word lid!
→ C nieuws
→ Nu op C
→ Over C
→ Links

→ C gids
→ C agenda

Zoek

---

**Lid worden is zo geregeld**

### C web-TV

**Rize**
Lorem ipsum dolor sit amet, consectetuer adipiscing. Lorem ipsum dolor sit amet, consectetuer adipiscing.

> Meer TV-programma's

### C web-radio

**Programma titel**
Lorem ipsum dolor sit amet, consectetuer adipiscing.

**Lorem ipsum dolor sit amet**
Lorem ipsum dolor sit

**Lorem ipsum**
Lorem ipsum dolor sit amet, consectetuer adipiscing.

> Meer radio-programma's

### C nieuws

**Nieuws item titel**
08-08-2006 - Lorem ipsum dolor sit amet, consectetuer adipiscing elit. Integer sem pede. Pellentesque blandit blandit sem,
> Lees meer

**Nieuws item titel**
05-08-2006 - pede. Pellentesque blandit, diam ac accumsan vehicula.
> Lees meer

**Nieuws item titel**
07-07-2006 - pede. Pellentesque blandit, diam ac accumsan vehicula.
> Lees meer

> Meer nieuws

**Nieuwsbrief**

C heeft de sympathie en medewerking van o.a.:

CNO

> Meer sponsors

### C kunst en cultuur agenda

**Grachtenfestival**
*Stedelijk CS 12 Augustus*

**Rembrandt tentoonstelling**
*Rijksmuseum 11 Augustus*

**Grachtenfestival**
*Stedelijk CS 12 Augustus*

### C kunst en cultuur gids

Lorem ipsum dolor sit amet, consectetuer adipiscing elit.

> Bekijk de C kunst en cultuur TV-gids
> Bekijk de C kunst en cultuur radio-gids

> Agenda

© C - omroep voor kunst en cultuur 2006 Pers | Contact | Disclaimer en privacyverklaring | RSS feeds

---

# EBGE

"Designersunited.gr" is a design group that was brought into being by acclaimed art directors Dimitris Koliadimas and Dimitris Papazoglou in order to engage visual research and systematic methodology into the design process. Founded in Thessaloniki Greece, and with the addition of brand strategist George Fassas in 2006, "du" creates print and digital graphics that enable businesses, art institutions and other organizations to improve and strengthen their visual identity by inventing an innovative and unique visual language.
In 2007 it became the first design studio to be awarded twice with the "Grand EBGE", Greece's top National Award for Design and Illustration.

TI: Art Design
DF: Designersunited.gr
AD: Dimitris Koliadimas
    Dimitris Papazoglou
CO: Greece
YP: 2007

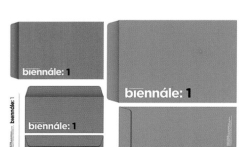

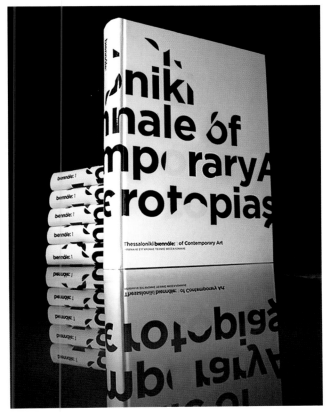

# Ceramic

Though the gimmicky marketing borders on greenwashing -- the refillable cups are definitely "greener" rather than out and out "green" -- this is certainly a step in the right direction for a pretty wasteful product.

TI: NOODLE CUP
DE: Adrian Allen

# Chocolate

Service by "Nieschlag + Wentrup": - Brand development (naming and label design) - Packaging for ten varieties of chocolate - Packaging for two varieties of coffee and prosecco labeling.

TI: Greta Gold - Fine Foods
CL: Greta Gold - Feine Kost
DF: Nieschlag und Wentrup
CD: Lisa Nieschlag Lars Wentrup
AD: Lisa Nieschlag Lars Wentrup
DE: Lisa Nieschlag Lars Wentrup
PH: Rasmus Schübel
CO: Germany

# Dog

I just saw this posted on NOTCOT and had to share. Designers Nina Dautzenberg and Andrea Gadesmann of Berlin-based JungeSchactel have done the unthinkable. They've managed to take a mundane (and unpleasant) task and make it fashionable and eco-friendly. So get rid of those landfill clogging plastic bags, and pick up a box of these 100% biodegradable, 100% adorable, poo bags. Aside from the cute illustrations, fun color palette, and humorous sayings... the product design is innovative as well. With a built in "scoop" these are certain to make the task at hand a bit more sanitary.

TI: Dog Poo Bags
YP: 2008

## dog poo bags

# Pizza

Eatablished in 1963, Pizza Nova is a family-ownsd corportion of over 100 outlets. While the growing chain operates in the highly competitive fast-food sector, they have never compromised the quality of their product. As the next generation takes over the stewardship of the company, Pizza Nova felt that their brand identity no longer effectively represented the quality of thier product.

CL: Pizza Nova

# Bath

Joie, designed by
Matthew Stiffler of
Palatial Creative, is a
new boutique bath line
that is in development
and will soon be
available at retail.

TI: Joie
YP: 2008

Tapio, a new premium, all-natural blended spirit from the UK, designed by Transfer Studio. Tapio Ventures is a lifestyle company with strong ethical and sustainability policies. Its key brand, Tapio, is a spirit mixed drink made from all-natural ingredients. Transfer Studio was commissioned to create a brand identity that reflects the core values of the company and that

will be suitable for a range of products still under development. The design was kept simple and clean to allow for diversity and to provide a canvas for the brand to build upon as its product range grows.

TI: Tapio
YP: 2008

# Restaurant

Striking corporate
ID and packaging for
an Istanbul based
restaurant called
"Loop". Designed by
Sani Levi.

CL: Loop
DE: Sani Levi
YP: 2008

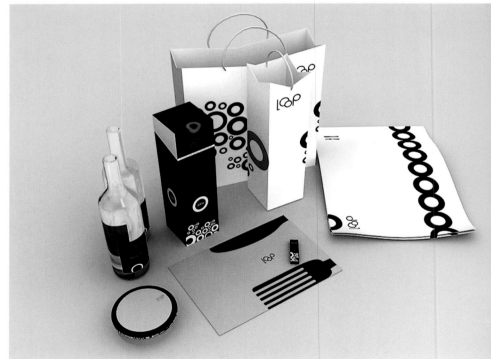

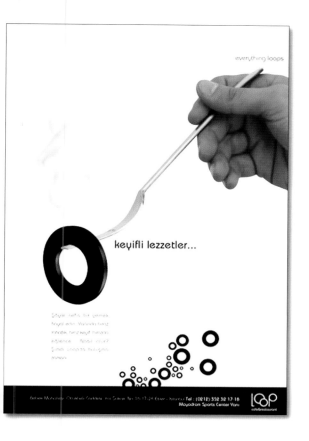

everything loops

keyifli lezzetler...

everything loops...

Loop
cafe&restaurant

İtalyan ve Kaliforniya mutfaklarının
eşsiz tatları Loop'un keyifli atmosferiyle buluştu.

23 Mart Toast Day

iki dilim arası lezzet!

4 Nisan C Vitamininin Keşfi

Hazır mısınız? Vitamin C keşfi başlıyor!

16 Mart Artichoke Hearts Day

lezzetin kalbinden gelen sağlık!

19 Mart Chocolate Caramel Day

Mutluluğun formülü!

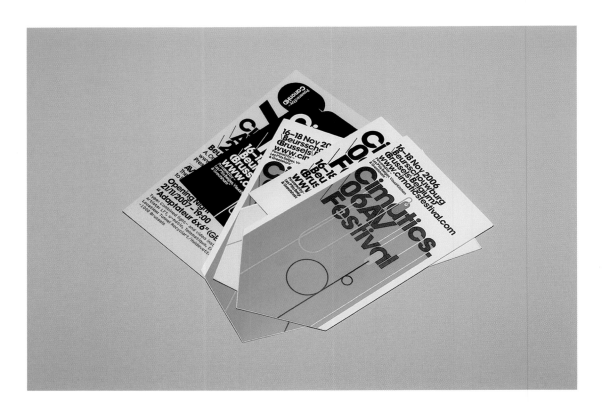

# Magazine

Magazine cover design
for the electronic
music publisher 'Cyclic
Defrost' (Sydney,
Australia). Includes
interview and various
pieces of work.

---

TI: 2007 illustration
    editorial magazine
CL: CYCLIC DEFROST
CO: UK
YP: 2007

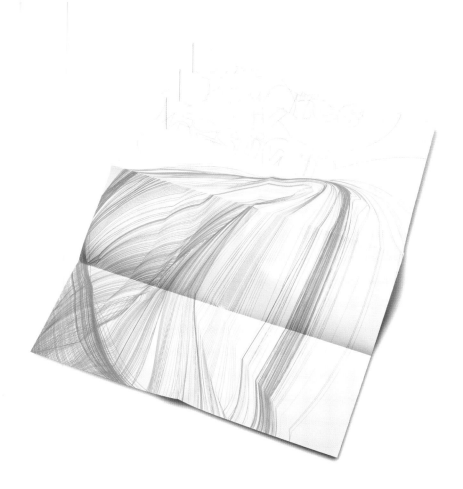

# Restaurant

Each year the festival
identity is changed/
tweaked to reflect the
festivals programme
for the year. Simple
striking 2 colour
design gets the festival
noticed. Design includes
- Programme design,
Posters & Signage.

TI: Cimatics AV Festival
CO: Belgium

# Restaurant

This Identity/
promotional work for
Cimatics AV Festival,
Brussels.
Each year the festival
identity is tweaked
based on the previous
years, building a
striking series. A bold
simple 2 colour design.
Collateral includes
- programme design,
posters & signage.

TI: CIMATICS 07 AV
    FESTIVAL
CO: Belgium
YP: 2007

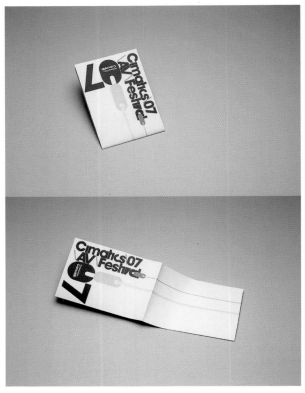

# Gift

This project for the Royal Festival Hall aimed at reintroducing a forgotten gift to the British people from the Indonesian people - the gamelan instrument. Our design included a recognisable visual language that would encourage visitors to participate and engage with the instrument and artists as well as an outdoor pavilion that would host a 48-hour jam session. Our approach was to rethink the boxes as a multiuse kit that lives beyond the event and is used for storage and transportation, but also functions as mobile seating that create meeting places and display information about the instruments.

CO: UK
TP: 2008

# Noble

MadeThought is a multi-
disciplinary design
consultancy adept in
brand identity and
development, art-
direction, packaging,
printed matter and
interactive design.

---

TI: Packaging
DF: MadeThought
Co: UK

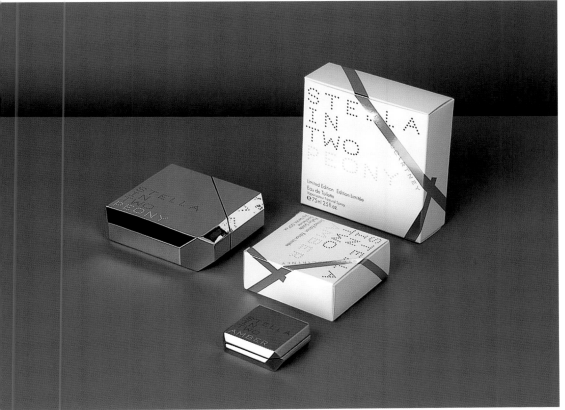

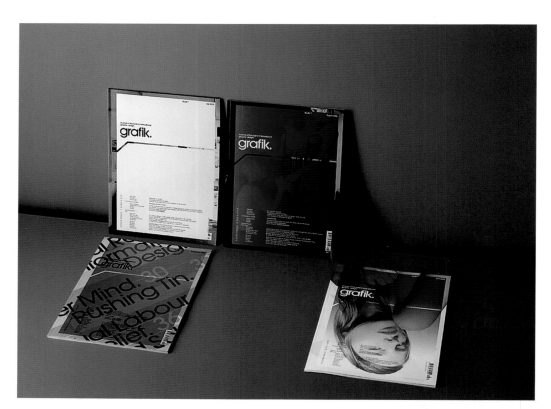

# Booklet

MADETHOUGHT Britain is
an integrated design
team, including many i▪
the field of design,
including products,
printing and so on, hi▪
work is very modern and
simple generosity.

TI: Grafik
DF: MadeThought
Co: UK

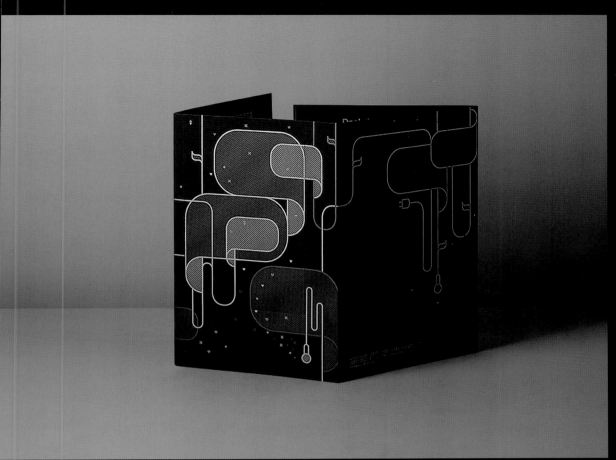

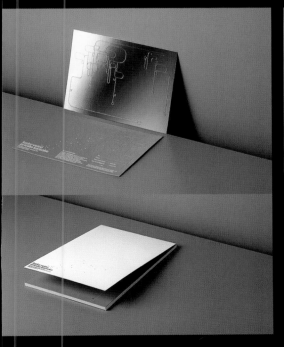

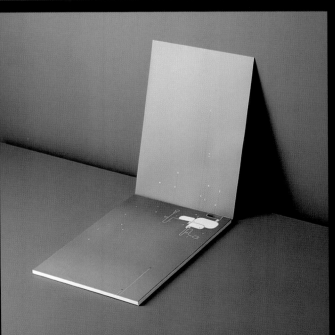

MCR/
Exten
TU-E1

Listen carefully...

MCR/NYC
Extended-Play Disc
TU-E17

MCR/
Exten
TU-E1

**SPA**

CL: WATER WOMAN SPA
DF: Harmony Design
    Adviser
CD: Yu Zhiwu
AD: Yu Zhiwu
DE: Yu Zhiwu
CO: China
YP: 2008

WATER WOMAN SPA
B Y   T H R E E

自然
Nature

# Commodity

CL: Azuma Commodity
DF: Harmony Design
    Adviser
CD: Yu Zhiwu
AD: Yu Zhiwu
DE: Yu Zhiwu
CO: China
YP: 2008

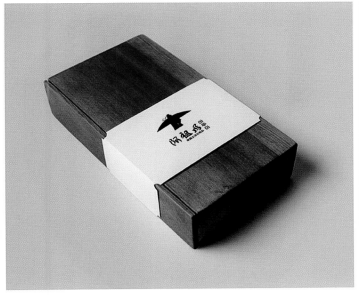

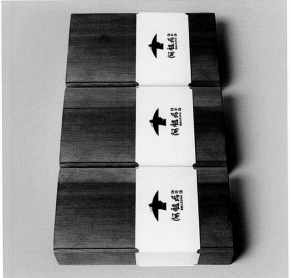

# Cookies

I love this aesthetic
— the juxtaposition of
white and red — the
pristine space. The logo
and its applications
are beautiful too.
Excellent work with air
as light, and space
as mood. Specially I
wondering for exciting
radiation of positive
energy and health that
coming from this works,
it's so need in time of
trashy style that we use
to see around. as for
me I prefer traditional
kind of beauty ...so
thanks for the good
work, it's really nice
to see and bon courage.

TI: GEMMA cucina
DF: On the table
YP: 2008

# Earth

This project is a social project and more then ever on the ravages of time. We didn't earn any money so far with doing that, but as the year 2008 is the "International year of Planet Earth" called out by the UN, we think, that all our efforts (blood, sweat and tears) did make and will make sense!

---

TI: Planet Earth - Directions for use
CL: Planet Earth
DF: Neongreen Network
CD: Angie Rattay
AD: Angie Rattay
DE: Angie Rattay
    Ulrich Einweg
CO: Austria

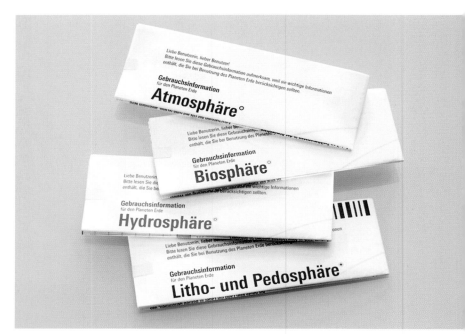

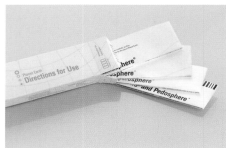

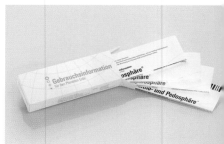

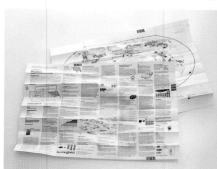

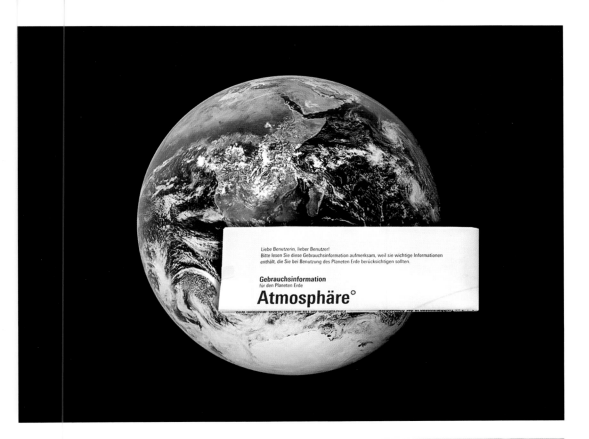

Liebe Benutzerin, lieber Benutzer!
Bitte lesen Sie diese Gebrauchsinformation aufmerksam, weil sie wichtige Informationen
enthält, die Sie bei Benutzung des Planeten Erde berücksichtigen sollten.

**Gebrauchsinformation**
für den Planeten Erde

# Atmosphäre°

Gebrauchsinformation
für den Planeten Erde

# Urbansilo

It's a storage facility
for work produced in the
past, and an incubator
for the culturing of
future ideas. It's
a work-in-progress
collection of concepts,
campaigns, experience,
taste, judgment and,
in some cases, 'pure
foolishness,' as Momma
would say. A nearly
100% organic blend of
rural roots, urban
insight and, hopefully,
zero horse manure. All
galvanized, pasteurized
and digitized for
maximum perusal and
pleasure. A place where
folks can visit, view
my wares and, if the
fit seems right, chew
the fat about a future
project. As a writer
and brand-builder by
trade and at the risk
of seeming a little
too big for my own
britches, Urban Silo
is a barefaced act of
self-brandalism.

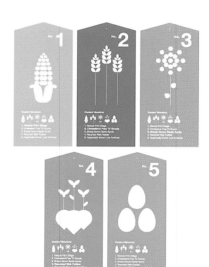

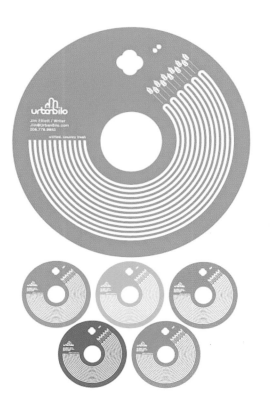

# Garden

TI: GARDEN OF WISH
DF: EMTC Advertising
CD: Lu HaiTong
AD: Lan Tian
DE: Lan Tian
CO: China
YP: 2007

# City

TI: STYLE YOUTH CITY
DF: EMTC Advertising
CD: Lu HaiTong
AD: Lan Tian
DE: Lan Tian
CO: China
YP: 2007

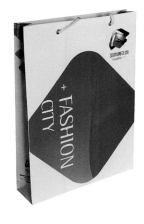

# Feeshy

TI: FEESHY
DF: EMTC Advertising
CD: Lu HaiTong
AD: Lan Tian
DE: Deng MingHui
CO: China
YP: 2007

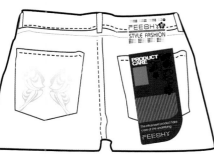

# Park

TI: QINGYANG LVZHOU
    PARK
DF: EMTC Advertising
CD: Lu HaiTong
AD: Lan Tian
DE: Lan Tiang
CO: China
YP: 2007

**青羊绿舟公园**
QINGYANG LVZHOU PARK
创意基地　光耀文明

**裴休·烟雨城**
PEIXIU · MISTY RAIN CITY
创意基地　光耀文明

**哈拉帕·醒城**
HARAPPA · AWAKECITY
创意基地　光耀文明

**青羊绿舟公园**
QINGYANG LVZHOU PARK
创意基地　光耀文明

**克诺索斯·幻城**
HARAPPA · AWAKECITY
创意基地　光耀文明

**马丘比丘·太阳城**
MACHU PICCHU · SUNCITY
创意基地　光耀文明

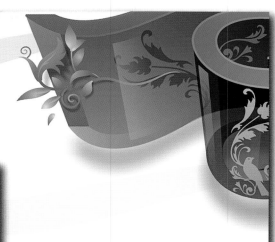

Before you begin using CorelDRAW, there are some areas with which you should become more familiar. To assist you in using the application, CorelDRAW provides several types of Help. When using CorelDRAW, you may find it useful to know the difference between vectors and bitmaps.

Furthermore, getting to know the various controls that appear in the application lets you work more effectively. Corel also provides several support services that can assist you with the application.

世界大隐　隐于成都①

**青羊绿舟公园**
QINGYANG LVZHOU PARK
创意基地　光耀文明

Furthermore, getting to know the various controls that appear in the application lets you work more effectively.

**青羊绿舟公园**
QINGYANG LVZHOU PARK
创意基地　光耀文明

**CONTRIBUTORS**

Corporate Indentity
has a high level of
understanding of the
enterprise will succeed.

Good Corporate Indentity
equivalent to the
marketing work has laid
a solid foundation.

Corporate Identity so
that the implementation
of enterprise information
dissemination
simplistic,
differentiated, easy
identification and
recognition of the
public, so as to achieve
the best communication
effect, do a good job
in public relations. At
the same time, Corporate
Identity itself created
by the excellent
corporate image, but
also the functioning of
public relations with a
solid foundation.

Long Gang
Li Jiong
Xia TianJian
Su Yi
Liu Ying
Liang Feng
Wang Hong
Wu WeiXi
RITO
Bao Bin
Hisen
Wang Song
Lai ZhaoYuan
Lu HaiTong
Simon Glover
Nick Stickland
Izvorka Juric
Carlotta Broglia
Alexis Rom
Claude Marzotto
Sander Tielen
Isidro Ferrer
Nicolás Sánchez
Nadine Häfner
Jennifer Staudacher
Kai Staudacher
David Stark Wilson
Creative Suitcase
Ivana Vucic
Orsat Frankovic

Key

TI: title
CL: client
DF: design firm/agency
CD: creative director
AD: art director
CW: copywriter
DE: designer
AU: author
PH: photographer
CO: country
YP: year of production

# BRANDING-AND-IDENTITY CONTEMPORARY GRAPHIC DESIGN 009-232

■
## It "sells itself."
## I don't need to market.

Okay, you might have a solid
product or service. You
might even routinely satisfy
your customers. They might
even send their friends and
family to you. But wait. Is
that your product or service
selling itself? No (that is,
unless your widgets have
learned to speak). That's one
of your customers playing
out-of-the-goodness-of-my-
heart salesperson for you.
Yeah, word-of-mouth is nice,
and if it's happening for
you, congratulations! It's a
sign of a great product or
service. But relying on it
exclusively can hurt you. Yes,
six degrees of separation and
all that, but counting on
those connecting conversations
to consistently mention you,
especially down the line, is
a bad gamble. Word of mouth
needs help.

A kick in the butt: a reminder
to your customers of their
good experience with you and
an enticing offer to potential
new customers to give you a
try. Providing this kick is
what a well-conceived branding
and marketing strategy should
do. At Brand Identity Guru,
we've got some BIG boots.

■
## "One of these things...
## looks just like the other"

You might sell red cars, and
Johnny Big Wheel down the
street might sell a similar
blue car. But what's under the
hood? Even better question:
what's under the hood that
makes yours better than the
blue car?

This is the essence of
differentiation in the
marketplace, and if you're
not playing up the things
about you that make you
different and better than your
competition, your marketing
is driving nowhere. At Brand
Identity Guru, we know how to
steer a marketing campaign
that leverages differentiation
to build your brand and

increase your bottom line.

■
## Liar, liar, your business is on fire and
## up and smoke

If you think word-of-mouth is
powerfully working for you,
it's just a fraction of the
punch a bad buzz can pack.
The best way to a bad buzz?
Over promising and under
delivering. It will kill you.
That's why it's important to
be truthful in your marketing.
Say what you can do. Not what
you wish you could do, or
might be able to do. If you
must err, do so on the side
of under promising and over
delivering.

■
## One-trick marketing is like a no-trick
## magician

It won't do anything, and
people won't pay to see your
show. To get your message to
resonate in the 21$^{st}$ century
market, you need to make
your appeal in every corner
the market looks. Print
advertising, direct mail,
online, telemarketing, public
relations, and in person. In
every place, a consistent
brand image and message.

■
## Microsoft Word clipart is for junior
## high book reports, not corporate
## identities

A logo is the face of your
company, so it must be unique
and memorable. Not available
for millions to place into
whatever bake sale flyer
they're working on at the
moment. But a corporate
identity is more than a logo.
It's your company's unique
value proposition and its
products and services?all
instantly recognizable on
sight of your logo, name and
tagline.

■
## Don't be visually absent

Talk can be cheap if it's not
paired with a strong visual
presence. Well-conceived
visuals connected with your
market makes your message

tick, no matter the medium.
rand Identity Guru is an
gency that can drench any
arketing effort with huge
ats of sticky visual honey,
ven if you're currently bone
ry.

## he typewriter and telegraph are cool achines, but not to use today

 business owner by nature has
o have a little bit of Evil
hievel in him, but when it
omes to technology, he or she
s often more of a cowardly
ion. That's understandable.
ou got into your business
ecause you know it, like
t and can put food on the
able with it. Not because
ou like to tinker with every
ew business technological
nnovation that comes down
he pike. However, cutting
dge technology can be a
owerful profit-generating
ool for your business,
specially when it comes to
arketing, and Brand Identity
uru, can help you find your
echnological sweet spot to
et your message out.

## an employee's 14-year-old son esigns your website, it will be ainfully obvious

 website must have a nice
ook, but that's a small part
f a good web presence. You
ave to give your prospect
nformation they need
nd close the sale fast.
therwise, they'll surf on by
o a competitor's website. In
oday's digital marketplace,
our website must be an
ntegral part of your overall
ales strategy. Not just a
oken presence. More than
ver, prospective customers
re researching their buying
ecisions on the web. If your
ite doesn't substantiate who
ou are and your offerings,
ducate, inspire and finally
otivate your visitors to buy,
our online presence isn't
trong enough. Brand Identity
uru, knows how to strengthen
t.

## ou have a website, but don't tell anybody

Having a website is pointless
if no one sees it. That's
why it's just as important
to drive traffic to your
website as it is to have one.
How do you do that? A great
way is through traditional
advertising like billboards,
print ads, signage and
printing the web address on
all your marketing collateral.
Online, there's search engine
optimization, banner ads,
online advertorials, keyword
purchases, links and cross-
promotion strategies. A good
mix of online and offline
traffic strategies along with
solid branding will drive
traffic to your website.

## "I don't need to be in the paper"

On the contrary, editorial
coverage carries more
credibility than any kind
of paid advertising you can
do. Getting it, however,
is difficult. Only a well-
conceived public relations
strategy that targets media
outlets your prospective
customers frequent will get
the job done. But it's not
just about writing press
releases. It's about providing
relevant information to the
media outlets you're trying
to get into and cultivating
relationships with key editors
and journalists. If you're
successful, you'll see your
name in print and a bigger
number on the bottom line.

## Branding done yourself is branding done badly

Given the choice of doing
branding yourself and not
doing it at all, you may
be better off not doing it
all. There are few things
worse for a business than an
"amateurish" image, and that's
usually the result with DIY
branding. Even if you know
how to do some graphic design
work or are a decent writer,
good branding takes strategic
know-how and the finesse and
time to get it just right-
things only a good branding

agency like Brand Identity
Guru can offer.

## If you think your employees aren't part of your brand? You're wrong.

Your brand is the face of your
company in every interaction
with the outside world, and
your employees interact with
it quite a bit. On the phone,
on sales calls, at schmoozing
and networking events, or
in informal settings, you
must train your employees to
represent your company in a
way consistent with its brand
image. Doing so can ensure
you have an army well-groomed
brand ambassadors out there.

## Failing to track your branding campaign's success can lead to future failure

If you don't make your
market's reaction to your
branding effort your business,
your business will suffer
mainly because you won't know
where to go next. Successful
branding is a constantly
evolving process, and if
you don't learn from your
mistakes, you'll continually
repeat them-and make more! On
the other hand, once you know
what your most successful
strategies are, you can build
off of them. Any branding
agency worth its salt will be
able to effectively track the
success of your campaign.

## Don't forget the clients who got you here, keep good relations

As businesses grow, they
sometimes forget the little
people who contributed to
their success. Don't. Those
who got you here can be an
invaluable resource to you
even if their business isn't
as important as it was. Since
they've known you for a long
time, they can offer valuable
counsel as to the future
direction your company, such
as offering their opinion on
new products or services. They
can also continue singing your
praises as another satisfied
customer.

This is not how to design a logo. This is a guide to educate you on how an experienced designer can help you through a project whose outcome you will need to live with for years. Learn how greatly the symbolic significance of your corporate identity can impact your Business. To say anyone can design a logo is to say anyone can design a story high rise. Here are some key lessons that will tell you if you're choosing the right architect for your corporate identity!

■
### Simple Definition- On The Surface

A logo design is composed of one or more elements of shape, type, and thematically chosen colors. In a glance, it conveys a substantial amount of information to the viewer, much in the form of short gut feelings that aren't vocalized -good, hesitant, authoritative, dignified, classy, upscale, expertise, cheap?the list is endless.

Your logo is a symbol that will stand on every piece of printed or electronic collateral for at least the next 10 years. Remember that thought. Changing your logo in a year because you don't like it breeds confusion and mistrust that spreads like weeds within your audience. Many people over look that fact when they have a logo designed from the Internet for $25.

Your identity is an extension of your Business that communicates visually, through appearance, and emotionally, through symbolism. Curtailing or ignoring thought, revision, and growth in the design process will hurt your finished product and corporate image. A good graphic artist will lead you through the design process. He or she will help visualize your company as the world sees you.

"I'm not creative," "I can't draw," "Make it green cause green is my favorite color and I'm the boss and it's my logo!" If you find yourself thinking along these lines, you're pretty normal so don't worry! If your passion and talent lie in matching the perfect violin to a young blossoming talent that walks into your music store, you're probably not going to do your own corporate tax returns.

Tax returns are done every year. Your logo, the heart and soul of your business is created once. It's part of you, and is the face of your Business the world will see. Let a graphic artist, whose own passion is design, help you with what they do best. It's well worth the investment. Let's look at why?

In the following we'll discuss some obvious and not so obvious things a logo communicates and illustrate by examples you'll recognize. You will have a greater understanding of how much power your little icon can potentially have.

■
### The Obvious Characteristics

From a usability and visibility standpoint there a several key factors that must be built into the design. Your logo must be clear and simple enough that it does not lose meaning when reproduced at different sizes, specifically smaller. If it is too cluttered and muddy on your Business card your first impression will be a disappointment to a potential client.

It must not lose meaning when reproduced in one color. The Internet and online marketing let you produce things in blazing colorful glory without extra cost. However, don't forget those equally important other places your logo will be seen like packaging, shopping bags, faxes, Xeroxes, newspapers, Business cards, brochures and letterhead. Those are important items in building brand loyalty and recognition to your product. If they don't look sharp, neither will your image, and neither will your sales.

■
### The Quiet, Harmonic Subtle Qualities Often Overlooked

Your logo is a symbol of your company's ideals, practices and missions. A well-developed, carefully sculpted logo can inspire vision, stability and comfort. Your image can make a viewer feel he or she is in the best, most experienced hands. With this visual interaction you are building a trust with your audience.

■
### Instill trust and a solid foundation

A logo can build trust and credibility. When you see a company's logo, even briefly you feel something. That something can make you uneasy and worried about what you'll get for your money, or it can make you feel safe. How about McDonald's? (Fat grams and calories aside for a moment) when you see the Golden Arches, most people think good, fun, always-know-what-to-expect-even-in-a-strange-land hamburger. If you are lost in a foreign country, sighting the McDonald's Logo creates a sense of familiarity and relief.

How about a black circle with two little circles on either side, toward the top. Mickey. (Yes, that might make some mom and dad's feel faint at the ticket prices), but beyond that, there's an unparalleled, magical feeling of childhood, laughter and joy. What powerful emotion from three, joined, black circles that transcends language and culture.

If we say your logo is a symbol, by definition it represents the heart and root system of your company. The ultimate goal is for your audience to feel and understand your Business on a

otional level and remember
. Sometimes logos can have
 abstract relationship,
metimes right in your face.
ther way, they must make
nse and uniquely tie into
ur Business. If you buy a
ir of sneakers with a swoosh
 them, do you have any
ubt that they will wear out
o soon, be uncomfortable,
 a waste of money?

## ow you are proactive and visionary

y you're in the market
r a luxury car. You are
obably less worried about
e obnoxious sales people and
re attune to advertising
u've seen. Which companies
mediately come to mind
en you think of precision,
rfection and technological
hievement?

gos like Jaguar, Mercedes,
 BMW convey enough inherent
nse of forward thinking
at they can appear as the
ly element on a billboard.
ere is a confidence you're
 a class of superior
gineering, advanced
chnology, and luxurious
yle compared to low and mid
nge automobiles. And even
re intriguing, if you're
 owner or in the market
r one, doesn't seeing that
rticular logo reinforce
ose ideals to you? How can
little silver kitty on the
ont of a hood evoke such
ep emotional reactions?

## rtray confidence and expertise

lvin Klein, Ralph Loren, and
ca-Cola are recognizable
om across a room. With
ch, you know purchased
oducts are consistent in
ality. I'd suggest the most
viously confident is Calvin
ein. But it works, doesn't
? The smell of CK cologne
ght trigger a good (maybe
d!) memory for you. Who in
al life is more confident
an the perfect underwear
dels that seem to be in
dless production? If they
n't radiate self-confidence
 that corporation, I'm at a

loss for what does!

People will argue Coke is
better than Pepsi or vice
versa. It really doesn't
matter because both are
regarded as the best cola
drinks made. Either one far
surpasses any of the knock
off brands. They are experts
in their field. So how does a
designer create an image like
these for your company?

How does a designer begin?
Every creative professional
has his or her own methods,
but the initial premise and
ultimate journey is the same.

## ◼ Design Is A Process

It is impossible to find
parallels of symbolism and
create a logo identity
without learning about the
company, interacting with its
employees, understanding the
products and services, and
examining the competition.

Here a designer starts to
understand what ideals
the corporate image must
convey and what makes the
company unique. Now, how to
communicate those thoughts,
feelings, and ideals onto
paper.

## ◼ Brainstorming/Draft

I usually carry a small
tablet around with me when I'm
working on a logo design. I
sit at lunch, at red lights,
and through the day sketching,
scribbling, jotting down
thoughts that pop into my
head. These aren't anything
for show, but quick ideas
that usually springboard to
new ones. Eventually one
common thread stands out and
I'll extrapolate some tighter
focused ideas around that
theme.

## ◼ Revision

This is the most important
process of design. This is
where shapes and words combine
into life. Here is where

ideas evolve into concrete
concepts. These concepts are
further reworked, poked and
prodded, transformed into
more detailed, individual
entities. A new idea may
still enter into the mix,
but results become much more
refined and defined.

At a point when gut instinct
and some outside opinions
say, "That's a keeper!" I'll
present the top three concepts
to the client. I may offer
some thoughts about color
or other added aesthetic
enhancements, but I'm more
interested in conveying the
underlying meaning of the
symbol, and how I think it
would speak to an audience and
drive the company forward.

## ◼ Conclusion

I strongly suggest you let an
experienced designer help you
with your logo development.
It's not unreasonable to pay
several thousand dollars for
a design. That design should,
however, take more than two
days to develop and a lot of
interaction and explanation!
But you have to live with the
results and they should be
nothing less than great.

When interviewing several
graphic artists, ask them how
they develop a logo. What
steps do they take? Their way
might be a bit different than
this article, but the general
thought should be the same.
You're Business is probably
your most valued investment.
Help the world believe that
too by having a logo that
conveys it.

Name recognition, building
trust, and brand loyalty take
time. All of the companies
talked about were new once
too. And, all are innovators
with their own unique,
wonderfully expressive faces
to the world.